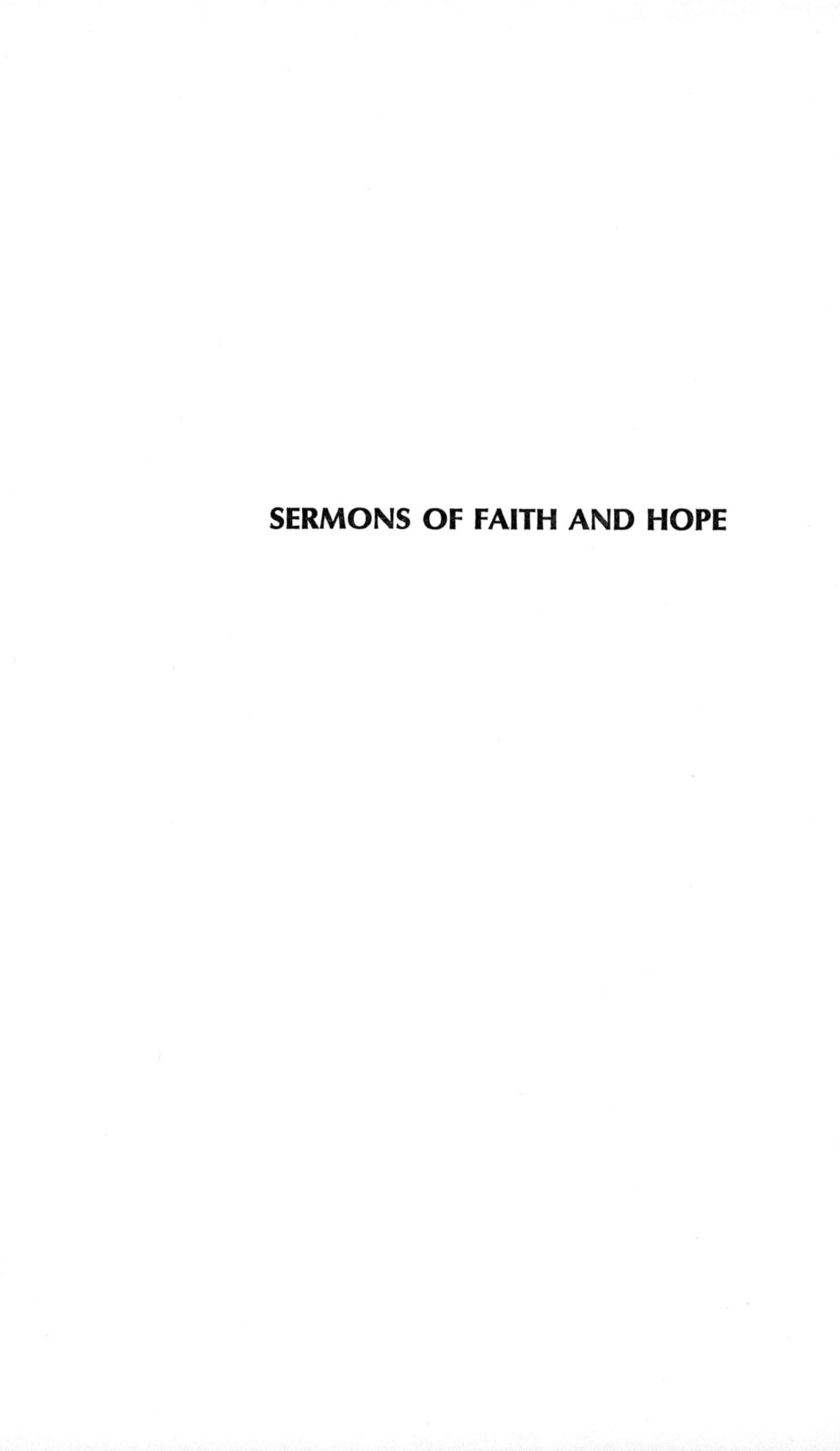

SERMONS OF FAITH AND HOPE

SERMONS OF FAITH AND HOPE

DAVID A. MacLENNAN

JUDSON PRESS
Valley Forge

To our Grandchildren
  Ann
  Bill
  Kathleen
  Kirk
  Margaret
  Mary Louise
  Paul
  Stephen
  Susan
  Thomas
with love and hope

CONTENTS

Lord Jesus, come into our minds to enlighten them; come into our hearts to cleanse them with thy love. Amen.

GOOD NEWS FOR YOU: MORE LIGHT THAN WE CAN LEARN
Part 1

The light shines in the darkness, and the darkness has never put it out. This was the real light, the light that comes into the world and shines on all men (John 1:5, 9, TEV).

One of the twentieth century's most frightening hours was unintentionally induced by a radio-broadcast play. It was produced by Orson Welles from a story by H. G. Wells. The story was science fiction. It depicted an invasion of our planet Earth by hostile beings from outer space. The sound effects and the acting of the players were so realistic that they produced panic in some communities. In that pretelevision era, listeners actually believed that the fantasy was fact. Many who heard the broadcast rushed into the streets and others took to the highways to escape the destruction they thought was imminent. It required official assurances over the entire network to inform the radio listeners that no such invasion had happened or was about to happen.

Simple, sturdy men who were looking after their sheep and lambs in Judean fields experienced emotions of fear and dread when an actual invasion of our world took place at the coming of Christ. Here is how Today's English Version of the New Testament described the experience:

"There were shepherds in that part of the country who were spending the night in the fields, taking care of their flocks. An angel of the Lord appeared to them, and the glory of the Lord shone over them. They were terribly afraid, but the angel said to them: 'Don't be afraid! For I am here with good news for you, which will bring great joy to all the people. This very night in David's town your Savior was born — Christ the Lord! This is what will prove it to you: you will find a baby wrapped in cloths and lying in a manger'" (Luke 2: 8-12, TEV).

"Don't be afraid! For I am here with good news for you." It is good news, the best news, the greatest news we could receive. Another Gospel writer, John, reflecting on the meaning of the divine invasion when Christ came, spoke of it as the coming of the light. The word "light" occurs twenty-one times in John's Gospel. Incarnation means illumination. When Jesus grew to manhood, he spoke twice of himself as the light of the world (see John 8:12; 9:5). Nineteen hundred years later a poet and playwright named Christopher Fry expressed some of the deep meanings of the Christ event in these lines:

> The darkest time in the year,
> The poorest place in the town,
> Cold, and a taste of fear,
> Man and woman alone,
> What can we hope for here?
> More light than we can learn,
> More wealth than we can treasure,
> More love than we can earn,
> More peace than we can measure,
> Because one child is born.[1]

Think with me now of the first of these consequences of Christ's coming: "More light than we can learn." Yes, says John, "This was the real light, the light that comes into the world and shines on all men." A few verses earlier John declares that this light not only dissolves darkness; it is inextinguishable: "The light shines in the darkness, and the darkness has never put it out."

[1] *McCall's,* December, 1968.

Think of it! "Because one child is born," born in "The darkest time in the year," light shines in the darkness of our human situation. In the Bible, as in at least one other religion which was influential at the time, Zoroastrianism, light is the symbol of God's nature and action. Light is also a symbol, or figure of speech, denoting truth and knowledge. One of the "ivy league" universities has as its motto the Latin words, *Lux et Veritas*, light and truth. They are virtually synonyms that mean truth. Because "one child is born" (that Jesus who grew to manhood) we have more light, more truth, and more insight into life's meaning, into our identity and value as persons, and into our duty and destiny.

This is "good news for you" in this particular hour of history. First, it is good news because *in the fact of Jesus Christ we have the key to the mystery of life*. It is a mystery not always "sweet," as the ballad in an old light opera went. Life's mystery can be sour, bitter, and depressing. What is life all about? That is the question each of us has asked at one time or another. Soon after World War II, Winston Churchill described Stalinist Russia as a puzzle wrapped in an enigma. In that hour the Soviet purpose and program seemed to be a mystery to the most astute and calm observers. To not a few young people — and older people also — life is like that. It seems like a blot or blank, an accident between two biological events — birth and death — on one of the lesser planets. But if Jesus Christ is a revelation of reality, as we believe him to be; if Christ is more than a collocation of atoms, if he is indeed the light of the world forever shining, then there is a living, purposeful, acting Power in the universe, in history, and in our human lives. "What is life?" asks Paul. "To me, it is Christ!" (Philippians 1:21, TEV). So, that Baby was the mind of God in whom and through whom the mystery of the infinite would eventually be disclosed. The light which Jesus brings is the light in the creation story of Genesis. In that inspired poem God moved upon the dark chaos and said, "Let there be light." God's light routed chaos. Jesus routs chaos in our minds and souls.

We have good news for you, good news for me, and for every one. "Because one child is born" we have "more light

than we can learn" *about our own identity and our own value.*
Of course we are kin to the animals. Of course men exhibit
traits of character like those of untamed tigers, apes, and
sometimes jackasses. We are creatures of the dust, but we are
also human beings made in the spiritual likeness of God. "We
are God's children now; it does not yet appear what we shall
be" (1 John 3:2) if we accept Christ's evaluation of ourselves.
Because we are sons and daughters of God, we must live that
way. True, we are physical beings with physical needs. We
are also emotional beings who have strange and sometimes
simple feelings. We have minds; we can think, plan, and
invent. We are also spiritual beings with needs that only the
Spirit can satisfy. "Hippie" flower children are, for the most
part, from middle-class and upper-middle-class homes. What
they are doing points to the kinds of needs that secure middle-
class comforts cannot satisfy. Being an older person, I do not
"dig" their selection of satisfactions, but I recognize their
hunger, their search.

To the physician we are patients, body-mind mechanisms;
to the salesman, manufacturer, and industrialist we are potential customers; to the military authorities young men are
potential fighting units; to the pastor and preacher we are
parishioners — past, present, and, hopefully, future! To the
unscrupulous, we are persons to be exploited.

But to Christ, we are God's own children, loved beyond
all understanding, for whom he died. Jesus was no romanti-
cist about us. From Bible study we realize that he knew
what was in man. He knew that men can lie; they called him
a glutton and a drunkard. He knew that men can be petty;
they found fault with him for healing on the sabbath. He
knew that men could be cruel; they crucified him. But no
one has come near Jesus in believing in your possibilities —
and mine, and everyman's. He believed that the weak could
become strong; that the man who is cheating on his wife and
family could become straight and loyal; that the despised,
the failure, and the broken could be made whole. Why? Because Jesus saw men and women as God's own children with
unlimited moral and spiritual possibilities. When the once-
famous Negro tenor, Roland Hayes, cabled his mother in

Georgia that he had been invited to sing before Britain's royal family, she replied, "Remember who you are!" A child of God, a Christian; be respectful, she was saying, but keep your dignity. Walk with kings but do not lose "the common touch."

We have more good news for you. We have "more light than we can learn" *about our duty and our destiny.* "Walk in the light, as he is in the light" (1 John 1:7). Today's English Version says: "If we live in the light — just as he is in the light — then we have fellowship with one another." Yes, an endless conflict continues between the forces of darkness and light. But if we keep our light shining, we shall know that "The light shines in the darkness, and the darkness has never put it out" (John 1:5, TEV). Jesus not only said that he was the light of the world, but he said that we are to be the light of the world. "Whoever follows me," he said, "will never walk in the darkness" (John 8:12, TEV). Will you follow him? Will you take his grace, his help, to let your light of faith, of hope, and of love keep shining? There will be "more light than we can learn" right to the end of life.

A little girl came home from Sunday church school and informed her family that the lesson "was all about a man who used to go for walks with God. His name was Enoch. One day they took a 'specially long walk. And they walked on and on, till at last God said to Enoch: 'Enoch, you must be tired; you had better just come in and stay.' And he went!" That was it. His friends did not worry about him. He was being looked after, all right. Why not walk with One today who knows the way, who is the Way, who will be your companion right to the very end? There will be tedious and tiring, and sometimes dangerous, routes, but always there will be God, and at the close of day a safe lodging and a divine Friend saying, "We have walked a long way together. You must be tired. Come in and rest."

PRAYER: Thanks be to thee who art the Light we need to walk in the light. Thanks be to thee that a Child was born who is the way, the truth, and the life, even Jesus Christ thy Son our Lord.

Prepare our hearts, Lord, to accept thy word. Silence in us any voice but thine own; through Jesus Christ our Lord. Amen.

GOOD NEWS FOR YOU: MORE WEALTH THAN WE CAN TREASURE Part 2

Do you remember the generosity of Jesus Christ, the Lord of us all? [For you know the grace of our Lord Jesus Christ, RSV.] He was rich beyond our telling, yet he became poor for your sakes so that his poverty might make you rich (2 Corinthians 8:9, Phillips).

Listen again to contemporary poet-playwright Christopher Fry:

> The darkest time in the year,
> The poorest place in the town,
> Cold, and a taste of fear,
> Man and woman alone,
> What can we hope for here?
> More light than we can learn,
> More wealth than we can treasure,
> More love than we can earn,
> More peace than we can measure,
> Because one child is born.[1]

The angel said to the Judean shepherds, and to us: "Don't be afraid! For I am here with good news for you, which will bring great joy to all the people . . . your Savior was born — Christ the Lord!" (Luke 2:10-11, TEV). "Because one child

[1] *McCall's,* December, 1968.

is born" — the child Jesus who grew to manhood and became the Savior of the world — we have "more wealth than we can treasure." Imagine! The acquisitive, the greedy man, the miser, would say, "There is not that much wealth." Yes, says the apostle Paul, there is; and it is for you. "Do you remember the generosity [the grace] of Jesus Christ, the Lord of us all? He was rich beyond our telling, yet he became poor for your sakes so that his poverty might make you rich" (2 Corinthians 8:9, Phillips).

"He was rich beyond our telling." For Paul, Christ had all the power, dignity, prestige, and privilege that we associate with God. For Paul, Christ's sacrifice did not begin on the cross. It did not begin even with his lowly birth in a stable-cave. It began in heaven. It began when he laid his glory by and consented to become truly man, subject to all human stresses, strains, and pains. The immediate occasion for Paul's writing was a stewardship campaign. He was appealing to Gentile Christians to come to the support of the mother church in Jerusalem. As we might say, he was launching a capital-funds campaign to help Christians who had fallen into poverty. His most powerful argument is the example of Jesus Christ. "Do you remember the grace — the uttermost self-giving of our Savior?" he asks.

"He was rich beyond our telling, yet he became poor for your sakes." The only way God can win our love is to love us and convince us of his love. He has done this, even though he himself suffered and must continue to suffer because of our blindness and self-will. Paul expresses it thus: "The divine nature was his from the first; yet he did not think to snatch at equality with God, but made himself nothing, assuming the nature of a slave" (Philippians 2:5-7, NEB). "Having become man, he humbled himself by living a life of utter obedience, even to the extent of dying [on the cross] *the death of a common criminal*" (Philippians 2:7-8, Phillips).

The purpose of it all was "that his poverty might make you rich." Rich in money, stocks, bonds, and real estate? Without despising money, would you not agree that true wealth is really of the Spirit? It consists of faith, love, and peace with God in the power of the indwelling Spirit. When we are reconciled to God, fully ourselves yet sharing his life, then "in every way [we are] enriched in him" (1 Corinthians 1:5). So enriched, we become generous in spirit, in giving ourselves and our substance to help others. We say with the ploughman who experienced the grace of Christ in John Masefield's poem, "The Everlasting Mercy," "I knew that Christ had given me birth to brother all the souls on earth." Someone said that "Francis of Assisi took all men to his heart because he saw in them the Christ to whom he owed everything." [2] Because God in Christ loves us, what must we do? We must love others with Christ's love. Because God loves us unconditionally, we should love others unconditionally. In other words, I cannot be a snob and be a Christian, too.

Professor Halford E. Luccock, who had a genius for uncovering unusual illustrations, was fond of telling what he or another labelled a modern parable. In heaven St. Peter was disturbed every morning because he encountered what seemed to him to be an invading host of undesirable characters. He was sure that he had never admitted them through the regular procedures. Some of these people had never been baptized; others were totally ignorant of the most elementary knowledge of the Bible; and many had souls so damaged that they hardly merited a place in the celestial precincts. Determined to learn how they had evaded the regular process, the former "Big Fisherman" prowled around the walls of the celestial realm. At last he found a corner where a few stones had been removed since his last inspection. Even while he was there, a crowd was slipping through the opening. Ready to confront them with indignation, he found that the Lord Jesus was actually helping some of the crippled and infirm to make their way through the wall. "I'm sorry, Peter," Jesus said, "I know that this is against the rules and these poor souls are not all they should be. All of them are miserable sinners, but they are among my special friends and I want them here."

You know the grace, the generous love, of our Lord Jesus

---

[2] James Reid, *The Interpreter's Bible* (Nashville: Abingdon Press, 1956), vol. 10, p. 368.

Christ. "He was rich beyond our telling, yet he became poor for your sakes so that his poverty might make you rich." What shall we render to the Lord for all his benefits? We will take the cup of salvation. More, we will give ourselves with our gifts. We will love one another — all sorts and conditions of men and women — with something of Christ's love.

PRAYER: To him who loves us and freed us from our sins with his life's blood, who made of us a royal house, to serve as the priests of his God and Father — to him be glory and dominion for ever and ever! Amen.

Through the speaking and hearing of the Word,
work a miracle of renewal in us, O God, through
Christ. Amen.

GOOD NEWS FOR YOU:
MORE LOVE THAN WE CAN EARN
Part 3

*"To us, the greatest demonstration of God's love for us has been
his sending his only Son into the world to give us life through him.
We see real love, not in the fact that we loved God, but that he
loved us and sent his Son to make personal atonement for our sins.
If God loved us as much as that, surely we, in our turn, should love
one another! (1 John 4:9-11, Phillips).*

"Don't be afraid" — of being alone, of being rejected, of the
failures, and because of the sins you have committed. "Don't
be afraid!" said the angel. "I am here with good news for you,
which will bring great joy to all the people. This very night
in David's town your Savior was born — Christ the Lord!"
(Luke 2:10-11, TEV).

But "what can we hope for here?" asked Christopher Fry
in his verse:

> The darkest time in the year,
> The poorest place in the town,
> Cold, and a taste of fear,
> Man and woman alone,
> What can we hope for here?
> More light than we can learn,
> More wealth than we can treasure,

More love than we can earn,
More peace than we can measure,
Because one child is born.[1]

The last five lines express the tremendous affirmation at the very center of the Christian faith. Do you feel the wonder of it? "Because one child is born," and that child is Jesus the Christ, we have "more love than we can earn." Why does the coming of Christ make available, and even prove, that we have dealings with "more love than we can earn?" Well, a skeptic in argumentative mood might say, "Of course, genuine love of one person for another is something I suppose no one can earn. You can only buy the counterfeit. You can get something like it by bribes called gifts, perhaps." To which a clue to the answer may be found in the story told some years back by a Christian missionary in Africa. Before Christmas arrived, this missionary told his young students that on Christmas, Christians gave one another presents. These gifts, he explained, were an expression of the joy that had come to them because God gave us Christ to be our Savior and Lord and Friend. On the very next Christmas morning, one of the Africans brought the missionary a seashell of lustrous beauty. He was asked where he had discovered such an extraordinary shell. The native modestly replied that he had walked many miles to a certain bay, the only place for miles around that particular mission station where such a shell could be found. The teacher exclaimed, "My, I think it was wonderful of you to travel so far to get this lovely gift for me!" The African's eyes brightened as he answered, *"Long walk, part of gift!"*

Do we ever make a generous response to life without what may be described as "long walk" — effort, self-giving, self-denial, sacrifice? Christmas began with a "long walk." Can we not see the significance, as a friend of mine has suggested, that in the symbolism of the whole Christmas story there is one "long walk" after another? For example there was the long walk of Mary and Joseph to Bethlehem, the long walk of the wise men from the far country, and the long walk of the

---

[1] *McCall's*, December, 1968.

Holy Family as they fled for their lives far down into Egyptland. What shall we say of the long walk to Calvary, where it seemed to most people who knew about it at the time that the cross of execution marked the end of Jesus' long walk? But when you let the whole event and its inner meanings "grab" you, you realize that all this long walk was a part of God's gift.

In 1 John 4:9 we read: "To us, the greatest demonstration of God's love for us has been his sending his only Son into the world to give us life through him. We see real love, not in the fact that we loved God, but that he loved us and sent his Son to make personal atonement for our sins. If God loved us as much as that, surely we, in our turn, should love one another!'" (Phillips).

We know that there is in this universe, in our human situation, "more love than we can earn" because of God's unsurpassed gift. *The incarnation of God in the person of Jesus Christ is the demonstration of that love.* J. B. Phillips actually uses the word "demonstration" in his translation: "To us, the greatest demonstration of God's love for us has been his sending his only Son into the world to give us life through him." Today's English Version translates it: "This is how God showed his love for us: he sent his only Son into the world that we might have life through him." Another translation has it: "For God is love; and his love was disclosed to us in this, that he sent his only Son into the world to bring us life. The love I speak of is not our love for God, but the love he showed to us in sending his Son as the remedy for the defilement of our sins" (verses 9-10, NEB).

According to Henry Sloane Coffin, a Jewish schoolteacher with a brilliant mind, who was reared in an Orthodox Jewish synagogue, was on the staff of a teachers' college. She passed from Judaism to the Ethical Society in search of a more credible faith. Within a few months she lost by death both her mother and her fiancé. In her loneliness she found the Ethical Society to be very bleak. She began to attend Protestant church services with a colleague. After some months she sought out the minister and said to him: "I see it now." "See what?" he asked. "I see that what I admire in the

20

Highest is all there in Jesus and what I need God for Jesus does for me." In nontechnical language that is the Christian doctrine of the incarnation. This is what Christmas is all about. "The Word became flesh and dwelt among us." Why? That we might have life, that we might have the remedy for the defilement of our sins. God clothed himself not with language but with life. Christ is more than God's messenger to our world; Christ is God's message, his self-expression.

Yes, we have "more love than we can earn." The incarnation is the demonstration.

The incarnation — the coming of God in all his holy love, justice, compassion, and wisdom — when accepted, means what the gospel and our fathers knew to be salvation. Love alone can deliver us from the power of evil. Love alone casts out fear. But this love, so much "more than we can earn," in its living demonstration in Christ, *lays upon us an obligation.* What is this obligation? Hear the Scripture again: "If God loved us as much as that, surely we, in our turn, should love one another!" (1 John 4:11, Phillips). John then continues: "Though God has never been seen by any man, God himself dwells in us if we love one another; his love is brought to perfection within us" (1 John 4:12, NEB). Our human love is a response to divine love. "We love, because God first loved us." Love of God and love of man are connected inseparably. During Christmas 1968, this obligation came home to not a few as they watched Astronauts Borman, Anders, and Lovell make the Apollo 8 flight. On their incredible translunar voyage the astronauts aimed a television camera and sent back marvelous pictures of that heavenly body known as Earth. No man had ever seen it before because no man had ever left it before. As state after state and Canadian province after province vanished in cloud seas, the whole planet became a single, beautiful sphere. One of the ablest United Presbyterian laymen, Edward B. Lindaman of North American's Apollo Space Program, speaks of the effect of those views in his new exciting book *Space: A New Direction for Mankind:* "The sight sent many people to thinking one thought.

"The thought was best expressed, perhaps, by the poet

Archibald MacLeish: 'To see the Earth as it really is . . . is to see ourselves as riders on the Earth together, brothers on that bright loveliness in the eternal cold — brothers who know now they are truly brothers.' . . . A German lecturer in war studies at the University of London wrote: 'The remarkable pictures of the Earth taken from near the moon's surface impress on us the utter ridiculousness of the nature and substance of man's quarrels with man. . . .'" [2] Loving our neighbors as brothers and sisters means more than a kindly goodwill toward them. It involves paying increasing, immediate, radical attention to the correction of our relationship with our physical and material environment. If we do not do so we shall tomorrow starve to death from overpopulation, smother to death from air-pollution, or poison ourselves by polluting the plankton in our oceans and the water in our streams and rivers.

Yes, the space scientists, the geneticists, and other scientists are underlining the truth of Christ's gospel: that God's world and the solution of our vexatious problems require a new type of men and women. This new type of men and women I believe to be the persons who have responded to God's love in giving us Christ, by committing themselves to this love, by taking God's grace to live lives of Christlike love with others.

"Because one child is born" we have demonstration of God's love, "more love than we can earn." We have the obligation to love as he loved us. You know you can! Sometimes you do! All of us have received more than enough love to offer love to those who need it most.

One man tells of finding a bundle of letters in an attic. The letters were written by his grandmother to members of the family and friends shortly after the Civil War. Those were hard and bitter days, too — days filled with a great deal of hate and animosity. Many lives were made bleak and dark. Yet the man discovered that every letter ended with the phrase, "Have I told you lately what a wonderful person you

[2] Edward B. Lindaman, *Space: A New Direction for Mankind* (New York: Harper & Row, Publishers, 1969), p. 132.

really are?" Think of how those words would lift the recipient! God sent us a Gift wrapped up in a person, as though he were saying to us: "Have I told you lately what wonderful people you really are?"

PRAYER: How can we thank you for your wonderful love toward us in giving us and all your children the unsurpassed gift of yourself in Jesus Christ? We will welcome him into our lives and with your help love you and our fellow-souls of every race and class and condition, in Christ. Amen.

God of light, who sent a star to guide men to the place where Christ was born, guide us by the light of thy Word, that, delivered from darkness, we may offer him the gift of our lives. Amen.

GOOD NEWS FOR YOU: MORE PEACE THAN WE CAN MEASURE
Part 4

Don't worry over anything whatever; tell God every detail of your needs in earnest and thankful prayer, and the peace of God, which transcends human understanding [which is beyond our utmost understanding, NEB] will keep constant guard over your hearts and minds as they rest in Christ Jesus (Philippians 4:7, Phillips).

Thanks be to God for his gift beyond words! (2 Corinthians 9:15, NEB). Let us thank God for his priceless gift! (TEV).

John A. Davidson, a Canadian minister-journalist, relates this story: In a Christmas issue of a well-known overseas newspaper, a cartoon appeared with two foreground figures. The figures were Santa Claus and a small boy. Santa Claus has been reading to the boy from a book which he holds in his hands and which is entitled *The Christmas Story*. Santa Claus has a puzzled expression on his face as he looks at the boy. We can understand his puzzlement when we read the cartoon's caption, which indicates that the boy has just asked him, "And how did it end?"

In the background of the cartoon we find the answer to the boy's question. It is an answer which Santa Claus, the great modern symbol of sentimentalism and materialism, cannot give. It is a silhouette of a large cross with a man hanging on it. It's not very Christmasy, is it? It may even be in bad taste, according to our standards. My friend says it's like putting vinegar in eggnog. But a meaningful point is made by the cartoonist. The Christmas story cannot be isolated from the rest of the gospel of Jesus Christ. Of course, there is a place for sentiment in Christmas. It's a baby's birthday party! It is a time when not only boys and girls, but otherwise staid men and women, some of them grandparents and some great-grandparents, unbend and act like little children at their merriest. Nevertheless, it is not enough to concentrate attention on the baby Jesus. Always we must remember that the star of Bethlehem shines only by the light from Golgotha. A contemporary woman, Jean Burden, sensitive to this truth wrote:

> Because the cross
>   became a tree;
> because the rock
>   became a door;
> we celebrate
>   return to birth;
> we kneel upon
>   the humble floor.
>
> For this our shepherds
>   sing their hymns;
> for this our Wise Men
>   travel far;
> because the cross
>   became a tree;
> because the stone
>   became a star.[1]

God's good news for us and for all people is that the baby who was born in Bethlehem nineteen hundred years ago, was uniquely the Son of God's love, whose brief life did not end with his death on the cross. Because he lives, we, too, may live more abundantly. What does it mean to live more abundantly? What can we hope for here, as Christopher Fry asked in his verse?

[1] *Saturday Review of Literature*, Dec. 2, 1950. Copyright 1950 by The Saturday Review Association, Inc.

The darkest time in the year,
The poorest place in the town,
Cold, and a taste of fear,
Man and woman alone,
What can we hope for here?
More light than we can learn,
More wealth than we can treasure,
More love than we can earn,
More peace than we can measure,
Because one child is born.[2]

In his second communiqué to the young church in Corinth, the apostle Paul writes of mundane church matters, necessary but unexciting. Then he breaks out into a cheer: "Thanks be unto God for his unspeakable gift!" (2 Corinthians 9:15, KJV). "Unspeakable" may confuse us; better translations are: "Thanks be to God for his gift beyond words!" (NEB); "Let us thank God for his priceless gift!" (TEV).

But "more peace than we can measure"? Isn't this "putting us on"? Have there not been more wars in this tremendous twentieth century than in any other century that history has recorded? And the fighting, the wars, proceed even within the land we love — in the United States and Canada, between militant groups of minority and majority extremists; between the custodians of law and order and the despairing, the rebels, and the believers in violence. "More peace than we can measure?" More and more men and women are discovering, or rediscovering, that the truth of Christ, the peace among men of goodwill, is the only way that practical statesmanship must take if creative, just, and durable peace is to be built. Of course, the ending of war and violence is not simple. Most of us realize that there are economic and political factors, as well as psychological and sociological ones, which lead to war. The New Testament is the most hopeful book ever written. Realism is in it, but no hopelessness. Why? Because the Light has come, God's Light, and the darkness can never put it out. A baby was born and God is in control. Because one child is born, we cannot yield to unrelieved despair.

Do you recall reading of the year 1809, not much more than 160 years ago? In that year a pall of depression hung

[2] *McCall's*, December, 1968.

26

over Europe and North America. America was just beginning its existence and suffering an economic depression. All of the elements which led to the needless War of 1812 were in the picture. In Europe a ruthless, clever dictator named Napoleon Bonaparte stalked over the continent as Hitler almost did with his panzer units. Napoleon brought depression, terror, and desolation everywhere he went. It was a dreadful time. Yet in that year a child was born; in fact, several children were born who, when they became adults, brought hope and peace and light to men and women. Think of some of the children born in 1809! Abraham Lincoln, Prime Minister William Ewart Gladstone, Charles Darwin who opened an immense vista by his scientific research and theories, the poet Alfred Tennyson, the novelist Edgar Allen Poe, Cyrus McCormick who revolutionized agriculture, and Felix Mendelssohn, the composer of great music, to mention a few. Things were not as hopeless as many statesmen and preachers — wise men — must have thought in 1809. Why? Because God works through a child and changes society through children.

At Christmas 1968, the first astronauts landed on the moon and read the creation story as we know it in the Bible. Then Frank Borman signed off with a prayer: "O God . . . show us what each of us can do to set forth the coming of the day of universal peace." [3] I know how we are to begin. You know, too. We begin by accepting God's love, committing ourselves to that love as we know it in Christ. Then, having been reconciled to God, we shall work as being reconciled to one another in this redemptive, invincible love.

There will be no peace among nations without the dynamic, redemptive love which Christ personalized and let loose in the world. Bertrand Russell was not a Christian. Many regarded him as an atheist and a "Red." He wrote a book called *Why I Am Not a Christian.* Yet a few years ago he made an address at Columbia University in which he said that Christian love would provide "a motive for endurance, a guide to action, a reason for courage, and an imperative necessity for intellectual honesty." Of course, just repeating

[3] As quoted in Edward B. Lindaman, *Space: A New Direction for Mankind* (New York: Harper & Row, Publishers, 1969), p. 133.

"love is the only way" or exhorting us to "put a little love in your heart" will not bring peace to mankind. Statesmanship requires realism and, to use a blessed modern word, "expertise."

Meanwhile, you and I can have "more peace than we can measure." We can? Yes, you and I, despite all of our primitive urges, our competitiveness, our aggressive impulses and drives, and our emotional immaturity, can achieve deep inner serenity. When the first announcement was made to simple but intelligent folk on that Judean hillside, the angels sang:

> Glory to God in the highest heaven!
> And peace on earth to men
> with whom he is pleased!
> (Luke 2:14, TEV).

We have peace through the glory of God. We lift up our souls, our minds, our hearts to God. His glory comes first. Then human well-being follows. God's peace, the peace that "transcends human understanding," is more than being able to yawn, undisturbed by the claims of other human beings. For example, we may say when we lose a friend, "Oh, well, he's impossible. Forget it!" And again, when differences develop between ourselves and another member of the family, we may argue, "Why should I go on denying my own personality, foregoing my rights all the time?" But such attitudes lead to a dead-end road. The only road to reconciliation and peace is the road that is taken because on it God is glorified. Only when we are in tune with God's purpose demonstrated in Christ can we know deep, inner peace. We glorify God when we act always in the knowledge that all human beings, whatever their race or nation, also belong to God and are to be treated like members of his family. George Kaufman, the playwright, once confessed that he was an incurable optimist, but he "cured hard." He wrote that often when the telephone rang, he would rush to it, hoping it would carry good news for him, only to discover it was someone asking for a loan of money or else asking him to intercede to get a relative a job. "It took me a long time," he said, "to realize that people were not sitting around saying, 'What good thing, what wonderful thing, can we do for George Kaufman? Let's call him and tell him about it.'" Nobody was doing it.

The good news of the Incarnation is that God — the Eternal, the Divine Order, Wisdom, Power, Love — did just this. He thought out the glories, the goodness, the love we find in Jesus Christ, and said, "What wonderful thing can I do for those people? I will send them Jesus."

> What can we hope for here?
> More light than we can learn,
> More wealth than we can treasure,
> More love than we can earn,
> More peace than we can measure,
> Because one child is born.

Take this child. Enthrone him in your life. You will have something far deeper, far more satisfying than peace of mind. You will have the peace of pardon, of acceptance, of love, of hope, God's peace. "The peace of God, which is beyond our utmost understanding will keep guard over your hearts and your thoughts, in Christ Jesus" (Philippians 4:7, NEB).

PRAYER: Thanks be to thee, O God, for thy gift beyond words! Send us out to share thy gift with others through our more Christlike love, our living faith, our deathless hope, in Christ. Amen.

Direct our thinking, our speaking, our hearing, that we may fully know thee, and more completely love thee, through Jesus Christ our Lord. Amen.

WHAT'S NEW WITH YOU?

Therefore, if any one is in Christ, he is a new creation; the old has passed away, behold, the new has come. All this is from God (2 Corinthians 5:17-18).

When anyone is united to Christ, there is a new world; the old order has gone, and a new order has already begun (NEB).

Two acquaintances meet. They have not seen each other for a while. You can predict the remark: "What's new with you?" It is a good question to ask from time to time. Life, to deserve its name, must be marked by newness. Of course this does not mean wholesale disparagement or abandonment of all that is old. Not everything new is true or good. Not everything old is obsolete or worthless. Christianity holds fast to that which is good. No sensible person writes off a valuable heritage. One of the high services of the church has been to preserve moral and spiritual values tremendously worth preserving to give stability to life and society. The word "conservative" is not necessarily a synonym or the equivalent of "reactionary" or "obstructionist."

Nevertheless, what is new with you and me is immensely significant. The writer of the Bible's last book, The Revelation

30

to John, reported the creative purpose of the great God who operates ceaselessly within the universe and within his creatures' lives. "He who sat upon the throne said, 'Behold, I make all things new'" (Revelation 21:5). Frequently, religious forces are tempted to restore the past, to maintain the old regardless of its value for a changing time. Religious institutions and people sometimes fight with a blind fury to restore the kind of world that existed in men's minds before the challenges of Copernicus and Galileo, before Darwin, and before Freud. Such resistance is understandable. When we live in a swiftly changing time, with old landmarks vanishing, one radical change after another forced upon us, we indulge in sentimental longing for a familiar day. Nostalgia, longing for what is gone, may be a protective device against the pain of thinking.

Some years ago a Monday edition of a metropolitan newspaper reported this excerpt from a sermon: "Our fathers gave us a happy prosperous country. Instead of keeping it that way we became 'experts' in education, in nutrition, in housing, in welfare." (Evidently the preacher considered all these things abominations.) He went on: "Think of the years before the era of the 'experts,' a small town on Sunday, with everything closed down, everybody in church, hymns resounding down Main Street, the Sunday dinners. People in those days believed in paying their bills, and never thought of getting something for nothing or something that didn't belong to them." Does that bring tears to our eyes? If it does, we must be suffering from an allergy! When was the happy day to which that preacher looked back nostalgically? He may have been a youngster during the high days of Warren Gamaliel Harding. That time has been called "the age of the dinosaurs," the period of the greatest corruption in American history. Do you suppose that if we could get a hymn floating down Main Street in all cities and towns and suburbs, and everything closed tight as a drum on Sunday, all would be well? A friend called that kind of religion a Currier and Ives religion.[1] But the New Testament urges the idea of the new

[1] Halford Luccock, *Marching Off the Map* (New York: Harper & Row, Publishers, 1952), pp. 101-102.

covenant, new spirit, new heart, new creation, new earth, new obdience, new life, new bodies, new wine, and new wineskins.

Christians drink from something deeper than an old oaken bucket. Jesus said to the woman at the well in Samaria: "Whoever drinks of the water that I shall give him will never thirst; the water that I shall give him will become in him a spring of water welling up to eternal life" (John 4:14). Eternal life is life in depth, life vitalizing, renewing, re-creating. Adolf Hitler once unknowingly indicated the role of the Christian faith. (He did say a few true things; no one can be wrong all the time. Even a stopped clock is correct twice a day.) In *Mein Kampf* Hitler wrote that the revolution which he was preparing could be stopped only by those who brought against it "an explosive idea." The faith of Christ, and faith in Christ, will explode. Take the basic idea that God is our Father, the Father of all men. That idea can explode some of the hard, encrusted fallacies that we tend to hug to ourselves. Take the words "brother" and "sister," which have meaning as they are seen in the context of the fatherhood of God and the saviorhood of Christ. The idea explodes. Take the axiom that "he who takes the sword shall perish by the sword." We must let that explode in our minds and in government assemblies and offices if we are not to see most of our children and grandchildren explode in nuclear war.

Well, "What's new with you?"

First, *you are new!* If there is one unchanging fact about persons, it is that personality is always changing. True, some changes in our personality are not beneficial; they arouse concern in those who love us. But personality changes may be wonderful. Dr. Gordon Allport, late eminent Harvard psychologist, entitled a helpful study of human personality, *Becoming.* This is what you are, becoming something other than you have been. The basic pattern may remain, but within that pattern significant changes can take place. The astonishing newness of life which at our best we desire, is found through our trusting faith in Jesus Christ. Men and women, boys and girls, are changed into personalities that are much more unified, properly motivated, more dependable,

32

responsible, creative, and attractive. No one needs to remain as he is.

"Therefore, if any one is in Christ, he is a new creation; the old has passed away, behold, the new has come." What does it mean to be "in Christ?" What do we mean when we say a man or woman is "in politics," "in business," "in real estate," "in banking," "in photography"? We mean that such a person is immersed in it; he is enthusiastic about it; he finds in it his true vocation. He has made a particular kind of interest his ruling interest. He is committed to it. The person who is "in Christ" has made his decision for Christ. He is committed to Christ. Such a commitment releases power. J. B. Phillips translates Paul's phrase: "he becomes a new person altogether." Only an inner change can produce a changed person or a changed society. Exhortation fails without that inside job of transformation. The late H. G. Wells wrote that due to modern discoveries, inventions, and exploration, man had become a new animal. Yet, said Wells realistically, he goes on acting like the quarrelsome little ape he used to be. All Wells could think of was to shout at man, "Stop being an ape!" Shouting doesn't seem to manage it. The apostle Paul knew something that would change a man or woman: "if any one is in Christ, he is a new creation." What's new with you? You are new. You are in process of becoming what you really are intended to become.

What's new with us? If we are becoming new in our basic trust, our hope, our love — "in Christ" — it means that we can have *new relationships with others.* Paul speaks of the new regard for others he learned as he lived "in Christ": "With us therefore worldly standards have ceased to count in our estimate of any man" (2 Corinthians 5:16, NEB). Look at a person through the eyes of Jesus Christ and you get a true evaluation. From the Christian point of view, as contrasted with the prevalent human point of view, the significant thing about people is that they are *people* — not primarily Caucasian, Asian, African, European, nor North American, not rich nor poor. They are children of God. A neighbor said to a clergyman's son who was playing with a Jewish lad: "As a good Christian you must hate the Jews." The little fellow looked at the warped adult and said, "Jesus was a Jew, wasn't he?"

What's new with you? You, yourself, no matter the number of your birthdays. What's new? *Your relationship to reality, to God.* Your regard for other people, and therefore your new relationship to them. "A new commandment I give to you, that you love one another; even as I have loved you, that you also love one another" (John 13:34). You will desire the best even for the most repulsive, the most treacherous, the most troublesome person.

What's new with you? *The world, the situation we are likely to experience in the 1970's.* Fantastic are the previews in communication, transportation, space exploration, maintenance of healthful and decent environment, photo telephones, and an incredible new number of television channels with new receivers! David Sarnoff, to whom we owe so much of radio and television, at seventy-four years of age looked forward with eagerness to a wonderful world in which freight will be dispatched by guided missiles, oceans and continents will be spanned in three hours, hunger will be relieved, drudgery will be eliminated, and so-called incurable diseases will be cured by new procedures, drugs, and miracles in medicine and science.

As for space exploration, we know now that the sky is no longer the limit. Edward B. Lindaman, United Presbyterian layman, long associated with the space program, is author of the book *Space: A New Direction for Mankind.* In it, he has some wise words about what space may mean. "The triumphs of Apollo underline the irony that it is easier for man to go to the moon than to wipe out a slum, easier for him to coast through space than to clean up his own polluted skies, easier for him to manage cooperation in a vast technological enterprise than to forge brotherhood in a city block. Yet as man has conquered the seas, the mountains, and the air, he has also at each stage, in a small way, conquered part of himself. Therein lies the hope and the ultimate promise of his conquest of Space." [2]

[2] Edward B. Lindaman, *Space: A New Direction for Mankind* (New York: Harper & Row, Publishers, 1969), p. 28.

What's new with you? "He put a new song in my mouth,
a song of praise to our God" exclaimed the psalmist (Psalm
40:3). He had found life "really rough" but God has given
him newness of life. How will you enter life this coming year?
God's gift of pardon, love, and hope "in Christ" should put a
new song in our hearts, a new lift to our spirits. "What new
thing did Jesus bring?" asked Marcion, the second-century
heretic, of Irenaeus, a Christian leader. Answered Irenaeus:
"He brought all that was new in bringing himself." Let a song
rise in your souls!

PRAYER: O thou who makest all things new, enable us to
take newness of life which thou dost long to give. Send us
out to be free to live as sons and daughters of the Highest,
and to sing a new song of trust, of courage, of love, of hope.
For we would go into the future with Christ, and in Christ.
Amen.

Surprise us, O God, with new insights into thy truth, and into new wonder at thy love in Jesus Christ our Lord. Amen.

GETTING ON WITH THE JOB

I sent messengers to them, saying, "I am doing a great work and I cannot come down" (Nehemiah 6:3).

His mother said to the servants, "Do whatever he tells you" (John 2:5).

The sixth chapter of the book of the prophet Nehemiah tells about an ancient war of nerves, a cold war between the Israelites of long ago and their nearby enemies. Nehemiah was leading the Israelites in building a wall. Their enemies tried by various strategems and tricks to stop the construction and destroy the builders, just as Mr. Nasser of Egypt would have liked to see present-day Israel destroyed. The Arabs and others of that far-off time urged Nehemiah to engage in negotiations, to come down to where they were gathered for a private conference. It seemed innocent enough. Nehemiah saw through the stratagem, however. He "sent messengers to them, saying, 'I am doing a great work and I cannot come down.'" Four times the enemy teams tried to persuade him to join them and four times he refused "in the same manner."

What has this old story to say to you and me today?

A good citizen, and certainly *a Christian, must have a sense of social responsibility.* "I am doing a great work and I cannot come down" has sounded like a trumpet in many different centuries. These words have inspired and encouraged other persons in later crises. Some of us may recall Winston Churchill's broadcast appeal to us from blitzed England in the dark year 1940: "Give us the tools and we will finish the job." The famed Supreme Court Justice Oliver Wendell Holmes once declared: "It is required of a man that he should share the passion and action of his time, at the peril of being judged not to have lived."

Not only heads of state, leaders in the Christian church, and officials elected to positions of leadership need this summons. Whether we are retired from once-exacting responsibilities or continue to have them, we are involved in building some enterprise, contributing to a more decent and Christian community and nation. So many plausible appeals for our limited supply of time, attention, money, and energy are made to us; it is a great hour when we learn to say to secondary appeals: "I am doing a great work and I cannot come down."

Let me make a personal confession. In my undergraduate student days I was extroverting all over the campus and beyond it! I enjoyed extramural activities. We did not major in demonstrations or protests, but we had projects that consumed equivalent amounts of time and energy. For me, these included a stint of editing the undergraduate newspaper, participating in intercollegiate debating, acting in the university dramas, and briefly playing on a minor soccer team — until the coach located the team's weakness! In addition, necessity compelled me to earn money on weekends for tuition and board. Among the older men on the faculty was a learned, semi-retired professor, Andrew Browning Baird. To know him was to respect and admire him greatly. He was acting as librarian in the residential college where I lived. One day I brought him a little-used autograph album and asked for his signature and any word he wished to add. What he did brought me up with a jolt. For this noble man who never scolded, never reproached even rambunctious students, had evidently evaluated my situation. He wrote: "Keep your eye on the main issue." It was his way of saying, choose the top priorities and get on with the job.

Whether we are actively engaged in a profession or business or not, we have much to learn from the late Dr. Thomas A. Dooley, an eminent Christian, which is the important fact about anyone. As a young medical doctor he went directly from medical school into the United States Army, and reached North Vietnam in 1954. There he saw disease, famine, squalor, and death such as he had never seen. In 1956 his military service ended but unlike most of us he did not ask to be shipped home. He volunteered to lead a medical mission to a country (Laos) where there was precisely one fully trained physician for two million people. He went because he could not help it. It was the job he must do, and he got on with the job. Quite suddenly he discovered that what he had thought to be a harmless tumor on his chest was malignant cancer. In America he underwent surgery. In the hospital he dreamed of a ceremony that he had seen in Southeast Asia. It was the burning of the mountain. Before the monsoon rains the people burned the mountain because they thought, rightly, that the ashes would fertilize the soil for the planting of new rice. He knew what the dream meant for him. "I must," he wrote, "into the burnt soil of my personal mountain of sadness, plant the new seedlings of my life. . . . Whatever time was left, whether it was a year or a decade, would be more than just a duration. I would continue to help the clots and clusters of withered and wretched in Asia to the utmost of my ability. . . . Maybe I could now be tender in a better way." [1] So the young man, doomed to die, went back to Laos. Around his neck he wore a religious medal on the back of which were four lines by Robert Frost:

> The woods are lovely, dark and deep,
> But I have promises to keep,
> And miles to go before I sleep,
> And miles to go before I sleep. [2]

[1] Thomas A. Dooley, *The Night They Burned the Mountain* (New York: Farrar, Straus & Giroux, Inc., 1960), pp. 183-184.

[2] From "Stopping by Woods on a Snowy Evening" in *The Poetry of Robert Frost,* edited by Edward Connery Lathem. Copyright 1923 by Holt, Rinehart and Winston, Inc. Copyright 1951 by Robert Frost. Reprinted by permission of Holt, Rinehart and Winston, Inc.

He said, "If I stop now, I'll probably die sooner." He went back and worked twenty hours a day until he literally collapsed. He was doing a great work and would not come down until God's finger touched him and he slept to wake in Christ's nearer presence. On January 18, 1961, in New York, he died one day after his thirty-fourth birthday. He got on with his job. He did a great work. He obeyed what Mary, Jesus' mother, said to the servants at the wedding reception: "Do whatever he tells you."

In the face of death, we must get on with the job. Robert Louis Stevenson said that if you know you will never finish your folio, your book of your plans, get on with your page. I like what a woman novelist prayed: "Lord, give me work till my life is done and life till my work is done." Many people evade the job of helping Christ by evading the job of helping others, working for better government, providing more adequate education for God's children, striving for peace in the world, and ending all preventable distress, disease, and hunger.

A thoughtful layman finds these lines by an unknown author a needed reminder:

> He was going to be all that he wanted
>   to be—Tomorrow.
> None would be kinder or braver
>   than he—Tomorrow.
> A friend who was troubled and
>   weary he knew,
> Who'd be glad for a lift — and
>   who needed it, too —
> On him he would call and see what
>   he could do — Tomorrow.
> Each morning he stacked up the
>   letters he'd write — Tomorrow.
> And thought of the folks he would
>   fill with delight — Tomorrow.
> And hadn't one minute to stop on
>   his way —
> "More time I will have to give
>   others," he'd say — Tomorrow.
> The greatest of workers this man
>   would have been — Tomorrow.
> The world would have hailed him

had he ever seen — Tomorrow.
But, in fact, he passed on and
    faded from view.
And all that he left when living
    was through
Was a mountain of things he intended
    to do — Tomorrow.

(Author Unknown)

For success, get on with the job. You and I should accept the truth of the New Testament (see Matthew 25:14-29) that the reward of work well done is more work to do. When we rest on our oars and coast we get old too soon.

The same truth applies to grief and disappointment, also. To let sorrow work itself out requires the supplementary exercise of getting on with a helpful job. When her little daughter was killed, a woman named Josephine Butler engaged in work which made her one of the greatest reformers of her generation. When you witness to Christ, when your witness is in your life and service as well as in your words, you are doing a great work and you must not come down to completely boring inactivity and self-centered concerns. Whenever the Lord says to you to help him make the water of existence into the wine of joy for others, do it!

PRAYER: Our heavenly Father, save us for heaven's sake, and for earth's sake make us worth saving. Amen.

Uphold us who would uphold thee, O Lord, and give us insight into the truth in Jesus. Amen.

GOODNESS GRACIOUS!

Put on then, as God's chosen ones, holy and beloved, . . . kindness (Colossians 3:12).

Be kind to one another, tenderhearted, forgiving one another, as God in Christ forgave you (Ephesians 4:32).

"Goodness gracious!" It sounds like the exclamation of proper, "old-fashioned" people. The younger generation might say, "Sounds like real squares, if you ask us, which you probably won't!" Today, however, let me use the two words to ask a question: "Is our goodness gracious?" If it isn't, it may be the hard, legalistic type of goodness which causes critics to say, "He is good in the worst sense of the word."

A story about a famous prophet and one of the little-known persons in the Bible illustrates gracious goodness. You may read about it in the thirty-eighth chapter of the Book of Jeremiah. During a turbulent time in his nation, the prophet Jeremiah was arrested on the false charge of giving aid and comfort to the enemy. His enemies resented his realistic forecasts of national defeat and had him whipped and flung into a dry cistern, an improvised jail. "There was no water in the pit," says the record, "only mud, and Jeremiah sank in the mud" (Jeremiah 38:6, NEB). Then entered the little-known friend, an Ethiopian called Ebed-melech. Ebed-melech was a slave in the king's service. (God uses all types of persons as his agents. A friend observed that the first successful heart transplant ever made used the heart of a Negro, placed in the body of a Jewish man, by a white Gentile surgeon whose first name is Christian.) Ebed-melech pleaded with the king to let him rescue Jeremiah; otherwise the prophet would die from starvation. The king gave permission. He did more. He assigned three men to help Ebed-melech accomplish the rescue. Then, says the writer of this chapter, "Ebed-melech went to the palace with the men and took some tattered cast-off clothes from the wardrobe and let them down with ropes to Jeremiah in the pit. Ebed-melech the Cushite said to Jeremiah, 'Put these old clothes under your armpits to ease the ropes.' Jeremiah did this, and they pulled him up out of the pit with the ropes" (Jeremiah 38:11-13, NEB).

Note the thoughtfulness of this Ethiopian. He knew that Jeremiah, already weakened by his ordeal in the underground cistern, would be hurt further if he did not cushion the ropes with cloths. The Ethiopian was good, and his goodness was gracious.

Christians are those chosen by God to be kinder than necessary. We are to be, with God's help, as good as possible. But goodness which consists of keeping the Ten Commandments, trying to practice the ethics of Jesus, is not enough. Our goodness must be gracious. "Put on then, as God's chosen ones, . . . kindness," writes the apostle to the Colossian church. In Ephesians, chapter 4, there is the more explicit directive: "Be kind to one another, tenderhearted, forgiving one another, as God in Christ forgave you" (Ephesians 4:32). Another translation has it: "Be kind to one another; be understanding. Be as ready to forgive others as God for Christ's sake has forgiven you" (Phillips).

Why should our goodness be gracious? Think of some of the reasons.

For one thing, *we will never commend the Christian faith and life unless we are gracious in our goodness.* A famous president of Wellesley College in Massachusetts was Alice

Freeman Palmer. She once wrote that she had found herself working closely with other Christians who, she said, "were kind, but cold. There was no intentional freezing, but an absence of the sunshine which melts its own way." In his best-loved short story, the parable of the waiting father of the prodigal son, Jesus depicted a good but unattractive elder son. He was surely good; we have his own testimony to the fact. But his goodness was austere, hard; as one old preacher said, he was so cold you could skate around him. When his wayward brother was welcomed home with a great homecoming party, he "was so angry that he would not go into the house" (Luke 15:28, TEV). He, too, was in a far country because his goodness was unloving. A man once sent to meet a distinguished visitor asked, "What does he look like? How will I recognize him?" The answer came: "If you see a tall gentleman helping somebody, that will be Sir Bartel Frere." That should be the profile of every Christian, shouldn't it?

Why should our goodness be gracious? Another reason was given by a man named John Watson. Our parents or grandparents may have known him by his pen name, Ian MacLaren, a writer of homespun and often unforgettable fiction. Watson said, *"let us be kind to one another, for most of us are fighting a hard battle."* Is that reason enough to be gracious in our goodness, to be kind to one another? The Hindu poet Rabindranath Tagore, became extremely annoyed when his servant, a fellow Indian, did not arrive on time one morning. As time went by, Tagore got madder by the minute. He thought of various kinds of punishment for the recreant staff member. He decided to turn him out, discharge him, fire him. At midday, the man finally made his appearance. Without a word, he proceeded to go about his duties as if all was as usual. He made breakfast and began to clean up. Tagore watched the perfomance with mounting rage. Finally he said it: "Drop everything and get out!" The man, however, continued to sweep, and after another few moments said with quiet dignity, "My little girl died last night."

It is said that the colorful revivalist Billy Sunday once wrote the mayor of a city in which he planned to hold a revival, requesting a list of people in need of special prayer. The mayor very obligingly sent him a copy of the city directory! We all stand in the need of prayer — and of some gracious goodness. Why? Because most of us are fighting a hard battle. Is it really true? A friend plays with this hypothetical idea: Say you took twenty-five persons whom you know or whose names you picked at random and sent each of them the same telegram: "Just to let you know I am thinking of you in your difficult situation." My friend who makes the suggestion is sure that most of the recipients would be able to figure out some cause for consolation that you must have had in mind. Most of them would probably acknowledge with thanks for your thoughtfulness.

What kind of hard battles? The stark kind of battle that comes with the message that a loved one is dead. The gnawing kind that little Richard described to his teacher on the first day of school. He looked so pale that she asked, "What is the matter, Richard? Are you homesick?" "No," replied Richard, "I'm not homesick. I'm *here sick.*" Think of some of the battles. Loneliness, the loss of a life partner through physical death or through the death of love, the battle against some kind of addiction, pretence, hypercriticism, or inferiority. The battle involved in making a tough decision. What of the ordeals of belief and disbelief? Whom shall we trust? What can we believe? Did you have any mottoes in your childhood home? I remember one that my father had on his study wall: "I shall pass this way but once. Any good that I can do, or any kindness that I can show to any human being, let me do it now. Let me not defer it, or neglect it; for I shall not pass this way again."

Is our goodness gracious?

Why should it be?

The basic reason is summed up by Paul. *"And be kind to one another, tenderhearted, forgiving one another, as God in Christ forgave you"* (Ephesians 4:32). In one sentence Paul defines the law of our personal relationships. What is the law? Just this: that we should treat others as Jesus Christ has treated us. You and I have been magnificently treated by God. We have been forgiven. We have been made members of the divine family. We know ourselves to be loved by the

44

Father. We are "builders of tomorrow, children of the cross and of the empty tomb." All of this God has done and is doing, and the purpose of his mighty acts is that you and I should be kind to one another. Gracious goodness!

PRAYER: O gracious God, give us thy grace that we may be a little kinder and a little blinder to the faults of those around us. Let us praise a little more. Let the understanding and kindness and love, that was in thy Son Jesus without limit, be in us also. Amen.

Prepare our minds and souls, O Lord, to receive your word. Let any wounds made by your truth be healed by your love, in Jesus Christ our Lord. Amen.

GOSSIP: HARMFUL AND HELPFUL

Words of thanksgiving and cursing pour out from the same mouth, my brothers! This should not happen! (James 8:10, TEV).

What's wrong with gossip? Doesn't everyone gossip now and then?

You may recall the apocryphal story of the three clergymen on vacation at a resort. They decided to confess their weaknesses or sins to each other. Said a good priest, "Well, because I am celibate — unmarried — when I am away from my parish, I enjoy the company of lovely attractive ladies." Said one Protestant pastor, "I admit that although my church is strongly opposed to gambling, when I get away, I like to place a few bets on a horse race or a dog race. After some moments the third pastor said, "My chief sin is gossip — and I can hardly wait to get out of here!"

Let me warn you at the beginning. If you get the message this morning, it will be this: *Gossip can be a destructive evil force. But gossip can be a constructive power for good.*

What do we mean by gossip? One dictionary defines it as "idle talk; trifling or groundless rumor . . . to talk idly, mostly about other people." You might wish to argue with the dictionary when it speaks of gossip as talking *idly!* Gossip and

46

gossipers seem to be among the busiest, most active elements in our society!

But cannot gossip be harmless? Certainly. A Danish explorer, Captain Mikkelsen, searching in the far North for the bodies of members of an ill-fated earlier expedition, was absent in the icy wastes for two and a half years. It was the year 1909. He was without radio communication with the outside world. He and his men risked death more than once. When they returned safely, he said that the greatest enemy was not the terrible cold or lack of provisions, but the awful silence of those snowy desolations. "Our only relief," he said, "was gossip."

Nevertheless, gossip can be despicable. It can be the weapon of an embittered, emotionally disturbed mind. Malicious, slandering gossip has been an instrument of murder, the murder of a person's reputation. Shakespeare's familiar lines deserve remembering:

> Who steals my purse steals trash; 'tis something, nothing;
> 'Twas mine, 'tis his, and has been slave to thousands
> But he that filches from me my good name
> Robs me of that which not enriches him
> And makes me poor indeed.

One brilliant literary man said that a gossip is "a beast of prey who does not even wait for the death of the victim he devours." This is why James wrote so strongly about the sins of the tongue used for unkind gossip: "What a huge stack of timber can be set ablaze by the tiniest spark! And the tongue is in effect a fire. . . . It pollutes our whole being; it keeps the wheel of our existence red-hot, and its flames are fed by hell. It is an intractable [restless] evil, charged with deadly venom. We use it to sing the praises of our Lord and Father, and we use it to invoke curses upon our fellow-men who are made in God's likeness" (James 3:5-6, 8-9, NEB). For Christians, James has the obvious word: "My brothers, this should not be so."

Jesus himself warned: "I tell you, on the day of judgment men will render account for every careless word they utter; for by your words you will be justified, and by your words you will be condemned" (Matthew 12:36-37).

Why do we engage in unkind and even in cruel gossip? The same passage in James points to one reason: "If you have bitter jealousy and selfish ambition in your hearts, do not boast and be false to the truth" (James 3:14). It is an unfortunate characteristic of our human nature that we feel we can push ourselves up in importance by pushing another down. Yes, the New Testament is right. Gossip can be a powerful destroyer. Like an uncontrolled prairie fire or forest fire, it ranges far and wide. No one can completely stop gossip.

> Three things come not back —
> the spent arrow, the spoken word,
> and the lost opportunity.

What can Christians do? They can resolve that they will *not* circulate rumors that are unkind and harmful to another's good name or peace of mind. Recall the signs which were posted in defense industries during World War II: "Careless talk can destroy a brave man's life." Members of Rotary Clubs will be interested to know the origin of their "Four-Way Test" on the things we think, say, or do may be a saying of a once-eminent Presbyterian minister, Alexander Whyte of St. George's West Church of Scotland, Edinburgh. Many years ago he said that all gossip should be subjected to three tests:

1. Is it true?
2. Is it necessary?
3. Is it kind?

The Rotarians' Four-Way Test is similar:

1. Is it the TRUTH?
2. Is it FAIR to all concerned?
3. Will it build GOODWILL and BETTER FRIENDSHIPS?
4. Will it be BENEFICIAL to all concerned?

One further step we may take as Christ's men and women. We can be guided by his rule of love. "Love is kind and envies no one. . . . Love keeps no score of wrongs; does not gloat over other men's sins, but delights in the truth" (1 Corinthians 13:4-6, NEB).

What if you and I are victims of untrue gossip? We cannot explain to everyone who has heard it. But we can remember, as the gifted Indiana novelist Booth Tarkington once wrote: "Gossip's a nasty thing, but it's sickly, and if people of good intentions will let it entirely alone, it will die, ninety-nine times out of a hundred." [1]

But gossip can be helpful! Think back to the original meaning of the word. A gossip was one who sponsored another in the name of God. In Old English the word was "god-sib," God and kin. Related to this is the word "sibling." So a gossip was a person who sponsored one who was to receive Christian baptism. An old history book said, "Queen Elizabeth accepted the office of gossip at the baptism of James VI of Scotland." This kind of gossip can advance the great cause of Christ.

A year or two ago, I heard on radio the quiet announcement, "Keep the rumor going that God is alive." If it is true, as it is, that unkind gossip can be a cause of pain, it is also true we can and should *gossip our Christian faith!* Paul blasted those who became idle "by gadding about from one house to another — and not merely idle but gossips and busybodies, repeating things they have no right to mention" (1 Timothy 5:13, Moffatt). But Paul would praise those who, like Stephen, gossiped about the Lord Jesus Christ until Saul the persecutor accepted Christ as his divine Commander and Savior and became Paul the apostle.

True, not everyone can be an elder, a trustee, a deacon, or an officer in the women's association or the church school. We can't all "ush" as ushers or "deac" as deacons, but we can tell one another what our Christian faith means to us. We can spread the word that our church is worth attending, that our worship and fellowship are spiritually and morally enriching. We can gossip that the church is alive, friendly, and Christian, and that whosoever will may come and be welcomed. Dr. John Mackay, President Emeritus of Princeton Seminary, wrote: "A friend from Chile told me some time ago that the reason Communists had been able to make such headway in that republic is that when they mingle with others in the

[1] Booth Tarkington, *The Magnificent Ambersons* (Garden City, N.Y.: Doubleday & Company, Inc., 1918), p. 321.

marketplace, *they gossip about their faith.*" This is the prime secret of success. You can gossip your Christian faith. By the responsible use of this power to gossip the good news, you can rout the "anarchs of the night," the enemies of Christ and the abundant life.

Members of various churches in Houston, Texas, recently were asked why they had chosen to worship where they did. Nine percent liked the looks of the building, 14 percent were loyal to a particular religious body, 18 percent found the location convenient, 3 percent liked the pastor, 22 percent had been attracted through their respect for certain members and 34 percent had been invited by friends and neighbors. In other words, 56 percent of the persons questioned had become members because of the direct influence of someone who belonged.

In a salesman's office was this sign: "Unseen and untold is unsold." It is true in the building up of Christ's church. We must see our "prospects," and tell them. Gossip the faith!

PRAYER: Let the words of our mouths and the meditations of our hearts be acceptable in thy sight, O Lord, our strength and our redeemer. Amen.

Let thy Word come to us with power and love,
even thy Word made personal: Jesus Christ our
Lord. Amen.

HAPPY ARE THE HELPLESS!

Happy are those who know they are spiritually poor: the Kingdom of heaven belongs to them! (Matthew 5:3, TEV).

Blessed are the poor in spirit, for theirs is the kingdom of heaven (Matthew 5:3).

"O the bliss of the man who has realized his own utter helplessness and his own utter inadequacy, and who has put his whole trust in God; for then he will humbly accept the will of God, and in so doing he will become a citizen of the kingdom of God" — William Barclay's interpretation of the beatitude's meaning.[1]

Examine the teachings of Jesus and you are likely to reach this conclusion: Jesus upsets the apple cart of our evaluations. A friend has noted, "We congratulate those who are privileged and we pity the deprived. The Lord of life congratulates those for whom life is hard enough to keep them humble, and pities those for whom life is easy enough to make them arrogant."

"Blessed are the poor in spirit."

[1] William Barclay, *The Beatitudes and The Lord's Prayer for Everyman* (New York: Harper & Row, Publishers, 1963), p. 28.

Would you make the first ingredient in a recipe for happiness that to be deeply, authentically happy you begin by being poor in spirit? Jesus spoke in Aramaic, the popular form of the Hebrew tongue in his land and time. The word he used, which is translated "poor," means *abject poverty*. The Hebrew word meant the helpless man, the man who could not put trust in himself or in his income, but only in God. It is the sort of poor man mentioned in Psalm 34:6: "This poor man cried, and the Lord heard him, and saved him out of all his troubles."

The term does *not* mean "Blessed are those who are economically poor," financially bankrupt. Jesus our Lord never praised such poverty. It is not a blessing to live in the slums, where health rots body and mind and decency struggles to keep alive. Christians must always aim to remove that kind of poverty. Samuel Johnson (1709-1784) expressed Christian sense when, two hundred years ago, he declared: "Poverty is a great enemy to human happiness; it certainly destroys liberty, and it makes some virtues impracticable, and others extremely difficult." Jesus did not mean that the lack of money or goods is in itself a blessing.

What kind of poverty, then, is a blessing and not a curse? Jesus says it is poverty of spirit. What does he mean? He does not mean poor-spirited, spineless. The pace of a Christian is not a crawl. It is clear from the total emphasis of Jesus that "Blessed are the poor in spirit" means "Blessed — happy — filled with bliss — is the man who realizes his own utter helplessness and puts his whole trust in God." In other words, the poor in spirit are those who are aware of their spiritual need.

Why is such a person fortunate? Why will he know a deep, abiding joy?

First, because he accents the fact of his own deep need. This is not easy for most of us. It is easier to recognize the needs of others. But the poor in spirit, in Jesus' meaning of the phrase, are the realists about themselves. They know that they have not the resources in themselves to meet life. Not the arrogant, nor the proud, but those who know their need are part of God's kingdom of vital and fulfilling life.

52

Did you hear of the boy to whom his father said in an unwise moment, "Son, I am largely a self-made man." To which the boy somewhat impolitely replied, "That's what I like about you, Dad, always taking the blame on yourself!"

But we should not be proud merely because we have or had sound nerves, intelligence, health, and a reasonably good up-bringing. We tend to be proud of our record and of ourselves, forgetting that most of our assets were not created by us. When the Judge of all the earth may ask us, "Well, what have you really done by yourself?" the honest answer can only be, "So little." If we have succeeded in any one of myriad ways, it is only because of the help of others, multitudes of them, known and unknown, and because God provided what we used for achievement. When we reflect on the mind, power, and wisdom of One who is our Creator, Provider, Sustainer, and Life Giver, how can we call ourselves self-made and be proud? As Frederick Meek, of Old South Church, Boston, once put it: "We are not self-sufficient for sixty seconds. We are always reaching out to take what He has provided: the lungs to take in air, the mouth to take in food, the ears to listen for sound, the eyes turning toward sights to be seen, the mind grasping for ideas, the heart yearning for love. And behind it all is God, the great Creator-Giver." [2]

The blessed person is like the member of Alcoholics Anonymous who knows he cannot make it on his own; the fortunate person is the one who acknowledges his need of a physician, a surgeon, or a Savior. Half the headaches and many of the heartaches are caused by halos that don't fit. The student who knows everything never learns anything. The alcoholic who insists that he can take it or leave it in his own strength, keeps on taking it and does not leave it. The busy executive who, during his days, finds no use for the living God, ends his days having made infinitesimal use of the life which God gave him in the first place.

Happy are those who have a keen sense of their need. They will move along the way to true power through realization of their helplessness.

[2] Frederick M. Meek, *The Life to Live* (New York: Oxford University Press, Inc., 1955), p. 8.

In the second place, *happy are the helpless for they learn to become detached from things.* One of the lilting songs of the last few years was sung by Julie Andrews in *The Sound of Music.* It is entitled "My Favorite Things." We need some things; it is enriching to have favorite things. Things may express our personality and not just our financial rating. But the Christian who knows the reality of his need, who has a sense of his moral and spiritual poverty, revalues wealth. We learn to become detached from things. Things cannot give deep happiness or security. When the chips are down, what is it we value most?

During the second world war, I read of a steamship torpedoed by a submarine in the North Atlantic in wintertime. Passengers were advised to take with them only what would help them to survive the rigors of an open boat in rough, cold weather. One woman said she rushed to her stateroom, deliberately left her jewel box, and brought a bag of oranges. Oranges, not diamonds and other gems, would be more valuable in the emergency. A more vivid illustration of what constitutes true values is in the record of the Shackleton expedition in the Antarctic. Members of the crew had to struggle across ice and snow to their ship. It was a long, cruel journey. They knew that they must travel light. Afterward, the men reported that they threw away their silver money and other impediments, and kept snapshots and other photographs of their dear ones.

Some of you may remember hearing of the conversation between two acquaintances when the newspaper reported the death of an unusually wealthy man. Said one: "How much did he leave?" Answer: "All of it." Robert Fontaine has told of two experiences in his life which demonstrated to him the value of choosing the most important things. When he was very young, one day he climbed as far up the steeple of the village church as he possibly could. He then found that he could not climb down again. The minister and the sexton had to rescue him with a ladder. When asked why he had ever done such a thing, he explained that he was simply trying to do what the minister had urged in his sermon. Fontaine had heard that God had created man a little lower than the angels and that if a man tried hard enough, he could reach any height.

Forty years later, Robert Fontaine said that he found himself in a hospital bed with a severe heart attack. With the thought of death ever present, he recalled that boyhood experience. He realized that instead of struggling and hoping and praying for the highest, he had settled for an easier goal. He had foolishly assumed that if he had the security and comfort of material things, he would have peace of mind.

But lying in his hospital bed, he realized that there was ever so much else to strive for, many more heights to reach, and that his chance to reach them might soon be ended. He resolved then and there that if he became strong again, he would never forget that he had indeed been made a little lower than the angels. He would remember that it was both his duty and his pleasure to aim at the moon. Even if he missed, as the Chinese proverb put it, his arrow would at least not go into the bushes. Happily, he had a chance to try again and no longer was content to seek the security of material things when he had a chance to clutch at a star.

Blessed is the person who is not possessed by his possessions. Happy is the man or woman who, while valuing lovely things, knows his limitations and puts his whole trust in God.

Once more: *Happy are those who realize their inadequacy, their insufficiency, their helplessness to live greatly — for they shall be linked and leagued with the great God of infinite resources.* God alone can bring us hope, health, and strength. As another said, "the way to [true] independence lies through dependence."

How does one reach that kingdom which Jesus called the kingdom of heaven or the kingdom of God? (Both phrases refer to the same realm.) Matthew, sensitive to Jewish readers, used "heaven" instead of the sacred name for God. The way begins with this first Beatitude. It does not express pious hopes for the future. The Beatitudes are congratulations on what *is*. A tourist driving along a New England road knew he was in the vicinity of Boston, but became confused as to direction and distance. He stopped to inquire of a country boy, saying: "Son, how far is it to Boston?" The boy replied, "Well, mister, if you keep going the way you're headed it's about twenty-five thousand miles. But if you'll just turn around and go the other way, you'll find Boston forty-six miles down this very road."

How far are you from a loving relationship with the living God? If some of us keep going the way we're headed, the way of superficial self-satisfaction that makes us confident we are wise enough to question the action and intention of anyone; if we are impelled to act like the Lord's attorney general and sit in judgment, or go the way of phony self-sufficiency, it's around the world, and around the world, and around the world again. But if we will just turn around and go the other way, the way Jesus showed and the way Jesus *is*, the way of those who feel their spiritual need, then it's really quite close. *In the very act of turning we are there!*

"O the bliss of the man who has realized his own utter helplessness and his own utter inadequacy, and who has put his whole trust in God; for then he will humbly accept the will of God, and in so doing he will become a citizen of the kingdom of God." [3]

PRAYER: Lord, help us to realize our own spiritual poverty and our own helplessness, and help us to come to thee that thou mayest make us rich in the things which really matter. For thy love's sake. Amen.

> He that is down needs fear no fall,
>   He that is low, no pride;
> He that is humble ever shall
>   Have God to be his guide.
>
> (John Bunyan)

[3] Barclay, *op. cit.*, p. 28.

Let our minds and souls be open to the leading of
thy Spirit, in Christ. Amen.

SEVEN CARDINAL VIRTUES: (1) WISDOM

*The wisdom that comes from God is first utterly pure, then peace-loving,
gentle, approachable, full of tolerant thoughts and kindly actions, with
no breath of favoritism or hint of hypocrisy. And the wise are peacemakers who go on quietly sowing for a harvest of righteousness — in
other people and in themselves (James 3:17-18, Phillips).*

Let me call to mind an inelegant comment that was popular
some years ago. It is sometimes heard even today. It is the
slang retort, "Don't be a wise guy!" By "wise" is meant something like another saying favored by the colloquially minded:
"Dumb like a fox." Today we mean much the same thing
when we say of a person, "He's a smooth operator." "Wise"
so used means shrewd, cunning, smart, clever. Yet Jesus said
that his followers are to be "wise as serpents and innocent as
doves" (Matthew 10:16). He also praised resourceful pagans,
the nonreligious, as in his parable where a crooked estate
manager received praise from his employer because he acted
shrewdly. "The children of this world," said Jesus, "are wiser
than the children of light." What did he mean? He meant
that if only the Christian was as astute, as resourceful, as in-
genious in attaining the good life as the clever secular man is
in his efforts to make money and attain the comforts of exis-

tence, the Christian would be more effective and a better person.

In the middle ages the undivided church drew up a list of seven cardinal virtues as well as a list of seven deadly sins. As you know, although we rarely use the word "cardinal" except to describe a bird, or a Roman Catholic ecclesiastic of high rank, or a player on the St. Louis baseball team, the word means the first, the most important. These virtues are wisdom, justice, temperance, courage, faith, hope, and love. Today, let us think of wisdom and how we may acquire it.

First, we know what wisdom is *not*. It is not equivalent to knowledge, or what we now speak of as "expertise." A person may be clever and well educated, and still be a fool. Jesus told a story of a man who cleverly manipulated the grain market. He was acquisitive, resourceful, and prudent. His profits were so satisfactory that he expanded his "plant." Then he heard God himself saying to him: "You fool!" He had put all his confidence in property, desirable as property may be. He was smart but not wise. Moreover, most of us know that much practical wisdom is bought at the considerable price of painful experience. A native of the state of Kentucky liked to tell of old Uncle Zeke in his hometown, who was celebrated for his wisdom. "Uncle Zeke," a young man once asked, "how does it come that you are so wise?" "Because," said the old man, "I've got good judgment. Good judgment comes from experience, and experience — well, that comes from poor judgment!"

One of the New Testament writers, the apostle James, had something to say about wisdom. James is the apostle of common sense. And in the letter that bears his name he said this, as J. B. Phillips translated the Greek:

"The wisdom that comes from God is first utterly pure, then peace-loving, gentle, approachable, full of tolerant thoughts and kindly actions, with no breath of favoritism or hint of hypocrisy. And the wise are peacemakers who go on quietly sowing for a harvest of righteousness — in other people and in themselves." (James 3:17-18).

The New Testament writer had true insight when he declared that *the source of true wisdom is the divine source of life and love*. "The wisdom that comes from God" (from "above," say the older versions). A few years ago a prominent British scientist, together with some of his scientific colleagues, came to the conclusion that scientists these days need something of an oath similar to the Hippocratic oath taken by medical doctors. Indeed, they went so far as to draw up a tentative one and it reads like this: "Realizing that my scientific knowledge provides me with increased powers over the forces of nature, I pledge myself to use this knowledge and power solely to what, according to my ability and judgment, I consider to be for the benefit of mankind, and to abstain from any scientific activity known to me to be intended for harmful purposes." Professor Coulson immediately adds: "Even such an oath, however seriously entered into, requires a point of reference against which to make one's judgment." That point of reference for C. A. Coulson is "the God of justice and righteousness, truth and love who communicated so vigorously through the prophets and who revealed his mind and spirit through Jesus Christ."[1] To be wise as well as smart requires a living, growing faith in that Wisdom and Love which is not ourselves, but which is the living God.

Many years ago a seminary student went to his first summer mission field in the Canadian northwest. He had come from the somewhat rarified atmosphere of Boston, Massachusetts. Out in ranching country, where the range had not yet been completely fenced, he encountered a few hardheaded and surprisingly intellectual skeptics. His own Christian beliefs were shaken. Fortunately for him his so-called supervising pastor was a man of culture and of tested Christian faith. When the young "sky-pilot" confided in the older man that so much modern science and the almost unanswerable logic of agnostics made him wonder if he could continue to represent the Christian cause, the older man told him of his own pilgrimage through doubt to a dynamic working faith in God and in Jesus Christ. "When I was an undergraduate, I too knew what it was to have my simple childhood faith almost wrecked. Someone told me that the university president was not only a working Christian but a man whose

---

[1] C. A. Coulson, *Science, Technology and the Christian* (London: The Methodist Book Room, n.d.), p. 41.

particular specialty had been in biblical studies. I somewhat timidly asked his secretary for an appointment. Gladly the president saw me and, as if he had no other duties, he listened to me. He answered many of my intellectual doubts, but he did something much more important. He said simply and convincingly, 'Every morning when I get up, I commit my own life, the day's duties and problems and opportunities, my dear ones, and this university into the keeping of the love and wisdom which I have experienced through simple trust in the God made known in Christ. I am sure that you can do the same.'" If so cultured and fine a man could live like that, the student reasoned, it was worth trying, and he did. He trusted what a poet called "the soul's invincible surmise." Life without knowledge is not worth living. Knowledge without love is not worth having. One of my friends says *It is never enough to love to learn; we must learn to love.* And the reason is that we are fulfilled not by what we know but by how effectively what we know enables us to relate to our source and to our destiny — God.

Love and peacemaking are essential elements of this wisdom which is from God. Our Scripture says that it is pure, cleansed of self-centeredness and the unworthy. Then it is "peace-loving, gentle, approachable, full of tolerant thoughts and kindly actions, with no breath of favoritism or hint of hypocrisy. And the wise are peacemakers who go on quietly sowing for a harvest of righteousness — in other people and in themselves."

In February, 1966, Rabbi Hillel Silverman, a former United States Navy chaplain, now the spiritual leader of Sinai Temple in Westwood, Los Angeles, preached in Westwood United Methodist Church. His theme was peace between persons, between differing religions, and between political and racial groups. He said that true brotherhood is the unity in diversity that makes America great, and that helping hand in cooperation and understanding. Then he told a true story. A few years ago in a northern Minnesota village a new family moved in. Their religion was a little different from the religion of the majority. If there was no prejudice in that small community, the new family nevertheless felt a wall separating them from the inhabitants. The people were cold, distant, suspicious. This new family did not feel very welcome until an unfortunate accident occurred. Late one afternoon, as the sun was setting, their six-year-old child wandered away from her back yard. They lived near a wheat field and the mother and father frantically began to search for their daughter there, but could not find her. It became colder. Then suddenly the neighbors began to appear. Neighbors they had not even met, Protestant, Catholic, and Jewish, came to help this family during their crisis. But all was to no avail. Finally, the mayor of the town said to them: *"Before it's too late, let's all join hands,* let's form an unbroken line, a human chain, and we will sweep this wheat field before it's too late. We will go up and down until we find the little girl." Sure enough, in thirty minutes they found her. She was half frozen but her heart was still beating. This girl lives today. Our rabbinical friend said: "I just cannot forget these words of the mayor, 'Let's all join hands before it's too late!' " We do face great challenges: war, secularism, ethical corrosion, Communism, exploitation, racism, and pollution of air, water, and all of our environment. We must join hands before it's too late. We can be wise as well as clever. To our knowledge we must add love, the love of Christ.

PRAYER: "God of grace and God of glory, On Thy people pour Thy power. . . . Grant us wisdom, Grant us courage, For the facing of this hour. . . . That we fail not man or Thee!"[2]

---

[2] From "God of Grace and God of Glory," by Harry Emerson Fosdick. Used by permission.

Stab our consciences broad awake with the truth,
O Spirit of love and truth. Through Christ. Amen.

SEVEN CARDINAL VIRTUES: (2) JUSTICE

Let justice roll down like waters, and righteousness like an everflowing stream (Amos 5:24).

I tell you, unless your righteousness exceeds that of the scribes and Pharisees, you will never enter the kingdom of heaven (Matthew 5:20).

I tell you that your goodness must be a far better thing than the goodness of the scribes and Pharisees before you can set foot in the kingdom of Heaven at all! (Phillips).

I tell you, unless you show yourselves far better men than the Pharisees and the doctors of the law, you can never enter the kingdom of Heaven (NEB).

I tell you, then, you will be able to enter the Kingdom of heaven only if your standard of life is far above the standard of the teachers of the Law and the Pharisees (TEV).

Does "justice" have a hard sound? No sensible person would deny that justice needs to be done if we are to live as human beings. Thirty years ago this nation joined Britain and France in fighting those whose injustice plunged millions into slavery and millions into death. Without justice — impartial, backed by law, enforced by adequate force — social order and the safety of citizens cannot exist. Moreover, the just person is the honest, dependable, responsible person. We do not wonder, then, that Christian leaders long ago placed justice high on the list of the most important qualities of character. Nevertheless, it sometimes has a harsh sound.

This cold and frigid aspect of justice is not softened by the equivalent word most commonly used in the Bible for it. Did you know that the word "justice" is not found in the New Testament, and is rarely found in the Old Testament? Where it is found it is usually translated "righteousness." Well, does this make the quality more appealing? When you picture "a righteous person," what do you think of? Someone who has all the qualities of a poker except its warmth? Someone like the elder brother in Jesus' famous parable of the prodigal sons — the icy regular, the faulty faultless prig who stayed at home and kept all the rules? Justice and the just person often look and sound rigid, frigid, and repelling. Even when we realize the tremendous value of justice, it is more honored in principle than in practice. Someone told of a devious character whose lawyer defended him in some court where the man could not be present for the final verdict. The attorney telegraphed him after he had won the verdict with the words: "Right triumphed." Back came a telegram from the client, "Appeal at once!"

When we think of *the righteousness of God,* as our forefathers did more frequently than we do, we tend to think of God's stern justice, his wrath against sinners. The God who has made himself known through prophets and all good men and women, whom we know as our heavenly Father through his self-disclosure in Jesus Christ, expects us to be just and good. This word comes through the great Old Testament prophets, such as Amos, Isaiah, and Ezekiel. Amos' report of the Almighty's demand is most familiar: "Let justice roll down like waters, and righteousness like an ever-flowing stream." God demands fairness between man and man. We are to be men and women of integrity. Jesus did not so much give rules of conduct as he emphasized the quality or the spirit of a person. He saw the Pharisees as being moral but not good. This is why he said, "Unless your righteousness exceeds that of the scribes and Pharisees, you will never enter the kingdom of heaven." I like Dr. Phillips' translation: "Your goodness must be a far better thing than the goodness of the scribes and Pharisees before you can set foot in the kingdom of Heaven at all!" Today's English Version also makes it clear: "You will be able to enter the Kingdom of heaven only if your standard of life is far above the standard of the teachers of the Law and the Pharisees."

A few years ago there was an unconventional preacher in our nation's capital, named A. Powell Davies. In a radio address he put it plainly: "If you are a nongambler and a teetotaler and at the same time put the rights of property before the rights of man, it might be better if you gambled recklessly and courted dipsomania if such course could leave you loyal to the principles of social righteousness and humanitarian justice. . . . What I am saying is that if you don't swear, don't cheat, don't lie, don't gamble, don't lose your temper, don't transgress any of these meritorious prohibitions and proscriptions, and yet refuse the claim of the world for brotherhood, the cry for a universal, just community, it would be better if you cheated, lied, and all the rest and still had room for the big claims, the great purposes of your age. What I am saying," he continued, "is that if you never listen to a dirty story but you do listen to race prejudice, you are far from pure. You are straining out the gnat and swallowing the camel. What I am saying is that petty pieties and paltry virtues are all too often a cloak, a mask, with which great sins are falsely compensated and disguised." But far earlier, when this Republic was young, Thomas Jefferson said: "I tremble for my country when I reflect that God is just."

But what can we do to be just? What must we do to be good? Hear again the good news. To begin with, it does not sound good. For the gospel of Christ declares that it is not in us to become good, to be just, to be better men and women. Again and again we have tried to obey a code, to follow rules. We have tried, and we have even cried out to be whatever God may be: "God knows I have tried!" The old Jewish Law (the Talmud) had 365 negative commandments, as many as the days of the year; and 248 positive commandments, as many as the bones in the body! But how futile is the effort to keep rules! Real righteousness, real justice, go far beyond trying to live up to a high personal standard.

True, rules and laws are essential, for, although we cannot legislate men and women into the kingdom of God, we can restrain the vicious, the criminal, and the morally and mentally sick from committing dreadful acts. Habits may be changed by legislative acts, judicial decisions, and executive orders. But more is required. How do we live above the average, and ahead of the crowd? Paul will tell you how. Innumerable men and women and boys and girls will tell you how. *You meet Jesus!* You welcome him, including his Spirit and his ethics, into your life. After the apostle Paul encountered Jesus and experienced the grace of Christ, he stopped struggling and striving to be morally good. No longer does the good man's righteousness end in self-righteousness. Why? Because he gives over, commits himself, to the love which reaches us through Christ. You and I must do this, too! Yes, you and I can say, "I give myself by faith to this same Love. I say 'I am not righteous and never can be, for righteousness belongs only to God. But perhaps I can keep the channel clear so that God can work through me!'" [1]

This is close to what the New Testament means when it speaks of being justified, accepted, and forgiven by faith, and given some of the justice, the goodness, the righteousness of God. Let me read Paul's words to the Roman Christians of long ago: "No man is put right in God's sight because he does what the Law requires; what the Law does is to make man know that he has sinned. But now God's way of putting men right with himself has been revealed, and it has nothing to do with law. The Law and the prophets gave their witness to it: God puts men right through their faith in Jesus Christ. God does this to all who believe in Christ, for there is no difference at all: all men have sinned and are far away from God's saving presence. But by the free gift of God's grace they are all put right with him through Christ Jesus, who sets them free" (Romans 3:20-24, TEV).

This does not absolve us from God's demand that we do

<hr>

[1] George A. Buttrick, *Sermons Preached in a University Church* (Nashville: Abingdon Press, 1959).

justly and love mercy and walk humbly before him. But it ends our striving. Out of sheer gratitude for being "put right" we take his grace to do justly and love mercy. Christ's judgment is clear and searching! "Not every one who says to me, 'Lord, Lord,' shall enter the kingdom of heaven, but he who does the will of my Father who is in heaven" (Matthew 7:21).

Why not begin to do his will where we live and work and play, by treating others fairly, with respect, and with Christ's kind of courtesy? Some years ago a man of small physical stature entered a motel. The motel operator was so unimpressed by his appearance that she told him she could not provide a room for that night. Her daughter came into the office at that moment, looked at the man, and recognized him. She quickly called her mother aside and whispered that the man she had turned away was a distinguished musician and conductor of a symphony orchestra. The motel operator called him back and offered all kinds of apologies. She said, "Why, of course we can take care of you. Why didn't you tell me you were somebody?" As the man turned angrily away from the desk and headed back to his car, he said to her, "Madame, *everybody is somebody.*"

PRAYER: O thou who art a just God and a Savior, thy justice is forever linked with thy love. Therefore we have hope; we confide ourselves to thee and take from thee wisdom and strength to do justly by others and by ourselves. In Christ our Lord. Amen.

May thy good Spirit guide us into the truth we need to live abundantly through Christ. Amen.

SEVEN CARDINAL VIRTUES: (3) TEMPERANCE

Let the older men know that they should be sober, high-principled, and temperate, sound in faith, in love, and in endurance. The older women, similarly, should be reverent in their bearing, not scandalmongers or slaves to strong drink; they must set a high standard, and school the younger women to be loving wives and mothers, temperate, chaste, and kind, busy at home, respecting the authority of their own husbands. Thus the Gospel will not be brought into disrepute. Urge the younger men, similarly, to be temperate in all things, and set them a good example yourself (Titus 2:1-7, NEB).

That's laying it on the line. The apostle is practical, as the gospel he preached is practical. He is comprehensive, issuing directives for good conduct to older men and women, younger women, and young men. True, his words to younger wives about subservience to husbands sound antique and obsolete. Such words might be resented and opposed by champions of feminism and equal rights for women today!

Paul's concern is that Christians live as Christians. Someone said recently that a Christian is the fifth, sixth, and seventh chapters of the Gospel according to Matthew walking down the street. The Epistle to a Christian named Titus stresses the word "temperate." The apostle Paul, when writing to the Galatian church, declares that one of the fruits of the Spirit of God, the Spirit of Christ, is, according to the King James Version, "temperance." What do the words "temperate" and "temperance" suggest to you?

One Christian whom I know always shied away from the word "temperance" because, as she said, she was not one of the "temperance people!" What she meant, of course, was that she was not a total abstainer. Neither Scripture nor the discipline of the church insists that members should be total abstainers from alcoholic beverages. Rightly, the Bible does take a dim view of those whom this Scripture passage calls "slaves to strong drink." Let no one treat excessive alcoholic drinking lightly. No one does who has had firsthand experience with it, either personally or with some member of his family. The story of the Irish priest who denounced it comes to mind. Preaching to his congregation in Ireland he said, "It's whiskey that's the bane of this congregation. It's whiskey that steals away a man's brains. It's whiskey that makes you shoot at landlords, and it's whiskey that makes you miss them!" Seriously, during the last twenty-five years scientific study of the effects of excessive drinking has shown how real and tragic is the problem. We have learned that alcoholism is a disease, and that the frequently fine men and women who go down under it need medical help, plus the help of vital faith in God, and the understanding help God gives through other men and women. To the AA's — *Alcoholics Anonymous* — thousands of persons owe an immense debt. It is unmistakably true that for some excellent persons total abstinence from alcoholic drinking is the only way.

It would be untrue to say that no sincere Christians temperately take a "social drink." The church does not forbid the wise use of any of God's gifts. In many of its branches, the church does preach temperance, but not total abstinence, except for persons who cannot handle any alcoholic beverage. A distinguished Scottish visitor told of his saintly father, an elder in the Scottish Kirk, who took a "wee dram" of whiskey from time to time. His son recalled how his father would bow his head in prayer before sipping the drink, thank God for all his gifts, and pray that he and others might never abuse or misuse any of them. So the church says, "Be temperate in all things."

Nevertheless, *"temperance" in the list of cardinal virtues means more than the ability to handle alcoholic beverages wisely.* In the Scriptures of our faith the word "temperance" is the equivalent of "self-control." Indeed, the Revised Standard Version and Today's English Version, the *New English Bible*, and the J. B. Phillips' translation have replaced the word "temperance" with "self-control." Paul, writing to Galatian Christians, lists among the activities of our lower nature, drunkenness. When he speaks of the harvest of the Spirit he writes of love, joy, peace, patience, kindness, goodness, faithfulness, humility, and *self-control.* There is no law against such things as these he declares.

Is self-control not needed in our generation, whatever part we play on the world's stage? Does not the wonderful God, whose we are and whom in our best moods we wish to serve, want us to be reasonable, self-controlled men and women? Do we not need such self-control as citizens? How easy it is to yield to the impassioned advocates of extremism, whether they be of the radical "left" or the radical "right." True, we need to be wholly committed to Christ, but such commitment and the enthusiasm that should go with it need not make us impetuous, unfair, angry, and hostile toward those who differ from us. Recently William Van Til, speaking at Indiana State University, said words which have relevance: "I often see," he said, "the angry bumper sticker reading: 'America — Love It or Leave It.' But I have not yet seen the constructive bumper sticker reading, *'America — Improve It or Lose It.'* Yet it seems to me the better way of showing your love for America is to improve it lest we lose it." Do we ever improve the nation we love by surrendering our confidence in "all that is true, all that is noble, all that is just and pure, all that is lovable and gracious, whatever is excellent and admirable"? (Phillipians 4:8, NEB).

How shall we be temperate men and women? Plato, the great pre-Christian philosopher, relied on reason, intelligence, and good sense. He was sure that, properly disciplined, the mind can move the will to avoid excess. Our valiant apostle

Paul also relied on intelligence and on his reason and will. Yet, realist that he was, he confessed that with his mind he wanted to do right — to be as an athlete in training — but his reason and his will let him down. Where did he find the master control? *In the Master.* Faith in Christ gave self-mastery. Faith in Christ, to use Paul's own words, enables one to be "strengthened with might by his Spirit in the inner man" (Ephesians 3:16, KJV). "The harvest of the Spirit is . . . self-control" (Galatians 5:22, NEB).

Our natural appetites are not evil. Our physical desires are not wicked. The body is God's temple because it is God's creation. Every instinct and every appetite of the body is good in its own place. What is evil is their perverted use, their misuse and abuse.

Jesus our Lord was no pale Galilean. Christ was no ascetic, spurning the innocent pleasures of life. Many of his followers have been. In nineteenth-century Scotland a young minister was brought before his Presbytery for skating on Sunday from one appointment to another. An elderly member of the Presbytery fixed a stern eye on him and demanded "Tell me, young man, did ye *enjoy* the skating?"

Yet self-control is essential. Even in little things it is good to do something useful or helpful every day for no other reason than we would rather not do it.

The season of Lent is much more than the time when, as a small boy said, "Episcopalians give up sin!" It is an opportunity to undertake discipline. "Discipline" comes from the same root as "disciple." "Disciple" means a learner.

Do we not need to practice helpful self-discipline? Dr. Benjamin Spock, once the advocate of permissiveness in rearing young children, now advocates reasonable discipline of youngsters and of adults on behalf of decent living. The Lenten season provides us with an opportunity to renew our prayer life, engage in a little self-denial, and become involved in greater service for Christ and his cause in the world.

You and I need a power greater than ourselves, the Power we know as God, as the living Christ, as the Holy Spirit. We, too, can be "strengthened with might by his Spirit in the inner man." Jesus Christ came to set captives free. Yet his first step was to bind them to himself. We are never really free until we are bound, voluntarily mastered by something greater than ourselves. George Matheson, Scottish poet-preacher, was minister of St. Cuthbert's Church of Scotland, Edinburgh. He was physically blind but possessed of rare insight into life's meaning and the Christian way. He wrote not only the hymn "O Love That Wilt Not Let Me Go" but also another great hymn included in most hymnbooks. Its opening line gives the clue to true temperance and self-control: "Make me a captive, Lord, And then I shall be free."

PRAYER: Lord of all life, we need the master control that commitment to Christ gives. Teach us that if thy Son shall make us free we shall be free indeed. For thy Love's sake we ask. Amen.

Capture our attention, O living Word of God, and make clear and convincing thy truth and love. In Jesus Christ. Amen.

SEVEN CARDINAL VIRTUES: (4) COURAGE

In the world you will have trouble. But courage! The victory is mine; I have conquered the world (John 16:33, NEB).

An observation was made in my hearing long ago. In the intervening years its truth has been verified by experience. It is this: "Courage is Fear that has said its prayers." Long after first hearing it, I came across the little verse, "Courage," from which it was taken, written by Karle Wilson Baker.

> Courage is armor
> A blind man wears;
> The calloused scar
> Of outlived despairs:
> Courage is Fear
> That has said its prayers.

Who would not agree with James M. Barrie in his famous address to students that "courage is the lovely virtue . . . courage is the thing. All goes if courage goes." Doubtless, an analysis of courage would show that a few persons have a kind of animal courage that has never known fear. Such a person is not to be envied. Without valid fear, a person would be prone to run headlong into avoidable danger. He

72

might incur injuries, sickness, or death. Healthy fear of disease has produced scientific medicine; fear of ignorance is responsible for schools, colleges, and universities; healthy fear — at least respect — for the sea, rivers, and lakes has led to greater safety measures in sailing, boating, and swimming. Fear of what pollution of water, air, and soil can do to human beings is leading scientists, government leaders, business men and women, and citizens generally to take constructive steps to reduce and to avoid continued pollution with its life-destroying effects. As for the fear of poverty, it has led to the organization of modern business and commerce, and to social security for the elderly and those unable to be gainfully employed. Fear of what moral failure and spiritual loss creates has often led to man's search for God and God's search for man, and God's costly gift of what the religious vocabulary calls salvation. Fear may play a useful, even a healthful, role. Courage is not the absence of fear; it is the control of it. Nevertheless, to live much with fear of vague enemies, to live in chronic anxiety, exacts a cruel price in physical, mental, and emotional health. To be mastered by fear is to be mastered by one of the most devilish forces.

It is courage that we need. We want the kind of courage that has mastered fears and weaknesses.

Jesus our Lord was completely human as he is mysteriously divine. As a human being who was "tempted" and "tested," as the Bible affirms, "in all points as we are," he must have known fear. He wanted his first followers not to fear the forces which could destroy their bodies, but to fear only the demonic powers which could destroy their real personalities, their souls. In one of his farewell talks with his inner circle of friends and pupils, John records him as responding to a confession that his first followers made to him. It was a confession of their faith, their great confidence in him. "Jesus answered, 'Do you now believe? [One recent translation is: "at the moment you believe."] Look, the hour is coming, has indeed already come, when you are all to be scattered, each to his home, leaving me alone.'" This would be a shattering announcement to them. "'Yet I am not alone,'" Jesus continued, "because the Father is with me. I have told you all this so that in me you may find peace. In the world you will have trouble. But courage! The victory is mine; I have conquered the world'" (John 16:31-33, NEB).

But had he? As far as anyone could judge his situation, he had not won any victory. He had not conquered that world in which corruption, greed, lust, and cruelty marked the human situation. The world of hostile men was closing in upon him. To be arrested, given a mockery of a trial, sentenced to sadistic scourging, then to death by crucifixion — a fiendishly cruel form of capital punishment — this is not exactly a victory, is it? But the verdict of the centuries is that Jesus had won the victory in advance. "He speaks as if the cross were already behind him — that cross in which he conquers the world by redeeming it and by defeating its diabolical ruler."[1] He had conquered fear, despair, and any sense of permanent defeat. On the battlefield of his soul he had fought the powers that can destroy the soul.

How can you and I attain courage like Christ's?

Christ told us.

First, we can face the worst and acknowledge that it is possible, even probable that we shall go through it. Jesus did. All truly brave men and women and boys and girls do. We live in a real world, and the dangers and risks are real. Jesus was the realist: "In the world you will have trouble." It is said that in that battle which was a complete mistake, the battle of Balaclava immortalized by Tennyson's poem "The Charge of the Light Brigade," a young cavalryman was heard to say when the order to charge was sounded, "Well, this is no girls' school so here goes the last of the Cardigans!" The heroism of ordinary people faced with what seem to observers to be impossible odds is one of the marvels of human existence. They make no room for self-pity. One instance is that of a boy named Ike Skelton, Jr. When he was stricken with polio as a young boy, a specialist told the parents, "If he gets better, healing will come from a higher Power than I." Months and years of painful recovery followed. It was in the days before

[1] A. M. Hunter, *The Cambridge Bible Commentary on the New English Bible. The Gospel According to John* (New York: Cambridge University Press, 1965), p. 159.

Salk vaccine. Seeing Ike's determination, the doctor changed his mind. He said, "Never have I seen such a will to win." Five years later Ike was a student at a military boys' school. He was on the track team. In the year's big meet he ran the two-mile race. His legs had recovered but his arms were still helpless. For the race his teammates taped his arms to his side. In the last lap Ike sprinted down the course. It made no difference that his opponents had finished two laps before. He gritted his teeth and tore across the line into the arms of his teammates. Said one, "The rest of them came in first, but they didn't beat that boy."

Here is a second tested way of developing this "lovely virtue," courage: *We can make Christ's faith our faith.* At the height of Jesus' final crisis, his closest friends left him alone. When the crowd came out armed with swords and cudgels, Matthew wrote: "Then the disciples all deserted him and ran away" (Matthew 26:56, NEB). But, deserted by men, Jesus was *not* alone. He had his Father's companionship. "You are all to be scattered, . . . leaving me alone. Yet I am not alone, because the Father is with me." This has always been his teaching, its purpose being to give his followers an inner resource. This is why the apostle Paul said, "God be praised, he gives us the victory through our Lord Jesus Christ" (1 Corinthians 15:57, NEB). He was speaking of Christ's triumph over the powers of evil in his death and resurrection.

Even more important, there is this further secret of courage: *you and I can enter into Christ.* Writing to the Colossian church, Paul wrote "The secret is this: Christ in you, the hope of a glory to come" (Colossians 1:27, NEB). William Law, onetime teacher of John Wesley, wrote: "This is the whole Gospel, the birth of the holy Jesus within us; His conquering life overcoming our inward death." He also said, "Christ not in us . . . is a Christ not ours." [2] Christ is to be a power within us, subduing our deep selfishness. Hear Christ's words again: "I have told you all this so that in me you may find peace. In the world you will have trouble. But courage! . . . I have conquered the world." "In me," he declares. In his company?

[2] William Law, *A Serious Call to a Devout and Holy Life* (New York: The Macmillan Company, 1898).

Yes. Courage is infectious just as fear is. "Christ's presence among you as your hope of glory" is Moffatt's translation of Colossians 1:27. But this relationship means more than to be in the company of Christ's men and women. We can have what an old-fashioned hymn describes as "mystic, sweet communion."

Is there more to this open secret of genuine courage? Yes. Recall the little poem's line, "Courage is Fear that has said its prayers." Prayer is power. Prayer releases acceptance, courage, and deep peace. "After these words Jesus looked up to heaven and said: 'Father, the hour has come. Glorify thy Son, that the Son may glorify thee'" (John 17:1, NEB). God glorifies his Son by sustaining him in courage. The Son glorifies the Father by the love and obedience that he offers. Then Jesus moved into what we call his great "high-priestly prayer" and prayed for others, "for those whom thou hast given me, because they belong to thee. . . . Holy Father, protect by the power of thy name those whom thou hast given me, that they may be one, as we are one" (John 17:9, 11, NEB).

> Courage is Fear
> That has said its prayers.

Now listen to a remarkable letter written by a young woman, twenty-seven years of age. A very effective pastor-preacher officiated at her marriage. Some years later he received this letter which he shared with me:

"I have been a sick girl for two and a half years. I was married only six months when I became ill. I was teaching physical education in high school. I went to several doctors and was treated for an ulcer for about one and a half years. Finally, when my condition grew out of hand, my doctor recommended me to a neurologist. He put me in a hospital right away and I had to take a leave of absence from school. He found I had a very large brain tumor for which a subsequent operation was necessary. The tumor had been growing for approximately twenty years; it was the size of a lemon and was located at the base of the brain against the medulla oblongata and its twelve nerves. I lost only two of the nerves — the seventh, facial expression, and the eighth, auditory. I am permanently deaf in my right ear, but partial movement of the right side of my face has been made possible by a nerve transplant. It took six months and seventeen days before movement in a corner of my drooping mouth was noticed. . . . Today I have fairly good facial symmetry when I talk, a slight smile, and it is possible to close my eye — all by manipulation of my tongue. At least I'm supposed to think I am manipulating my tongue.

"I went back to my first love of teaching in September, only to have to leave for further hospitalization in November. During my twenty-five-day stay in the hospital they found I had a severe case of endometriosis with many other internal complications. Following surgery for that, the climax came in the form of mental breakdown. I was on heavy drugs from November to April, when in desperation I volunteered myself as a patient in the State Hospital. I had become addicted! My stay there lasted only one and a half months, and I have now gained back not only my mind but my needed thirty-seven pounds. . . .

"Maybe this will help you to see, Dr. W., why I am still searching for the answer to 'Why?' I have not found it yet, but I have found something else. Do you remember a story you once told about an eccentric old Maine farmer and his fence? Like all his neighbors he built a stone fence. But his stone fence was unlike any that his neighbors built. For *he built his stone fence four feet high and six feet wide*. When his neighbors teased him saying, 'Why are you building such a wide fence?' he replied, '*So if it ever blows over, it'll be taller than it was before.*' It was this story that I clung to for dear life during all these months until, you know what, Dr. W.? I am almost certain I have become that stone fence. I am positive that I have been blown over, but I am just about as sure that I am taller than I was before."

The secret is honest facing of the facts, making Christ's faith your faith, living with Christ in you the hope of glory, and maintaining the prayer that lets God give you the gift of courage. You know the Power that enabled the young woman to win the victory. Now, through prayer, open your life to let that Power work in you.

PRAYER: O God, let Christ live in our souls by our trusting faith and obedience. So shall we be given courage to make experiments, and not to be afraid of making mistakes; courage to get up when we are down and to go on again; courage to endure what must be endured; courage to work with all our might for the coming of thy rule on earth, through Jesus Christ our Savior. Amen.

> Open our minds and souls to thy word for us,
> O God, and give us grace to receive and obey
> it, through Christ. Amen.

SEVEN CARDINAL VIRTUES: (5) FAITH

Set your troubled hearts at rest. Trust in God always; trust also in me (John 14:1, NEB).

One of the best-loved passages in the Bible is the fourteenth chapter of John's Gospel. Today, as in the centuries since it was written, it brings comfort to persons under stress. The first verse of the chapter must be familiar to millions: "Let not your hearts be troubled; believe in God, believe also in me." But the word "believe" suggests an intellectual act, a deliberate assent to a creedal statement. Beliefs are immensely important. A person would find it valuable to know the basic beliefs of anyone who employs him, of the person or persons from whom he buys property or services. To be able to say honestly, "I believe in God, the Father Almighty . . . and in Jesus Christ, His only Son our Lord" is one of life's most significant acts of faith. Nevertheless, when the Christian says "I believe," he means more than intellectual assent to a form of words, however majestic and profound. He means that he has vital faith in God.

But what is faith? It is easier to say what faith is not than to define clearly what it is. It is certainly not what a schoolboy said it was: "Believing what you know ain't so." Faith is not what Alice in Wonderland was told. When Alice did not believe some preposterous thing, she was told to shut her eyes, draw a deep breath, and try again. If I believe what one person is reported to believe, that drinking carrot juice will cause a third set of teeth to grow, that is not faith; it is superstition. What is faith? To be sure, faith is conviction that certain propositions or affirmations are true. Also, faith is the whole body of Christian truth. Perhaps a good working definition is this: Faith is trusting the whole of the personality to another, or to others. This is what is meant in the antique language of the marriage service, where both the man and the woman end their vows to each other by saying, "and thereto I plight thee my troth." "Troth" is the old word for "faith." Each of the parties to the marriage is saying to the other, "I pledge you my faith, my loyalty. I love you and therefore I trust you with my whole life." Christian faith is trusting in God made known in Jesus Christ, with the whole personality. To use a favorite word of younger people today, faith is *commitment* to this God.

To grasp more firmly the deep Christian meaning of faith, consider *Alice in Wonderland* again. Alice asked the Dodo, "What is a Caucus race?" She got the reply: "The best way to explain it is to do it." Do it they did. This is what the eleventh chapter of Hebrews does for us. That chapter begins with a definition of faith: "Faith means putting our full confidence in the things we hope for; it means being certain of things we cannot see" (Hebrews 11:1, Phillips). Then the writer proceeds to show faith in action. We are given a sight of famous Old Testament figures actually living by it.

Look at persons like ourselves living by faith in God.

Here is a woman overcome by real fear. She is Mary Mowat, a trained nurse, the matron of St. Peter's Hospital in the Stepney district of London, England. During World War II, air raids were all too common. Poor bedridden elderly patients occupied the top floor. When the sirens sounded and the bombs dropped or the V-1 or V-2 rockets exploded, these men and women who could not be moved were overwhelmed with terror. Their distress was pitiful. The matron, Mary

Mowat, entered at once and talked calmly to them, stealing away their terror. After the war she astonished one of her former patients by saying: "Oh, I was such a coward. When the raids began, my whole system seemed to collapse. I just stood up and said, 'Oh, God, You must do it. I am terrified, but You can save my poor patients in the top floor wards. Help them, Lord God; I cannot.'" Having offered her prayer, she went in calmly and pacified them all. She first made her own the deep peace Jesus offered and gives. "Set your troubled hearts at rest. Trust in God always; trust also in me."

Faith in God, faith in Christ is trust. To trust a bridge is to be willing to walk or drive across it. To trust the crew of an airplane and the aircraft's strength to withstand great stress is to board it. To trust God is to confide ourselves to God's wisdom, power, and love. "Faith means putting our full confidence in the things we hope for; it means being certain of things we cannot see."

Here is a man who is a good citizen of his country. He is troubled by what external enemies may do, and he is also disturbed by enemies of democracy and responsible freedom within. Just as you and I are made anxious by violence in the streets and defiance and ridicule of law courts and the judicial process, he is anxious. Then he remembers another citizen, a famous leader of the young republic of the United States of America. At eighty-one years of age, Benjamin Franklin reminded the members of the Constitutional Convention "We have been assured in the Sacred Writings, that 'except the Lord build the house, they labor in vain that build it.' I firmly believe this; and I also believe that without his concurring aid we shall succeed in this political building no better than the builders of Babel." [1]

Do your part, let me do mine, to remove causes of alienation by the young men and women and older persons who despise our constitution, our judicial system, and the rights of all persons to "life, liberty and the pursuit of happiness." Let us work as informed, resolute citizens to restore respect for just law and reasonable, necessary order. Then let Christ's

[1] Charles L. Wallis, *A Treasury of Sermon Illustrations* (Nashville: Abingdon Press, 1950), pp. 142-143.

injunction be obeyed by us: "Set your troubled hearts at rest. Trust in God always; trust also in me."

Here is a person worried about his health or the health of one who is dear and deeply loved. He goes to a physician, then perhaps to a surgeon whom he trusts. His trust in the doctor is a condition of cure. If this man learns that he has a critical illness, that his future may be precarious, he places his trust in the God of love, whose perfect will is for the healing and abundant life of all his children. He can say the words made familiar to many through the art work of the former nun, Sister Corita, who, since she left her Roman Catholic order, is known as the artist Corita Kent. Her favorite saying, first written by the Italian playwright Ugo Betti (1892-1953), was embodied in a painting which was reproduced on the February 15, 1970, cover of *Presbyterian Life:*

> To believe in God is to know
> that all the rules will
> be fair and that there will
> be wonderful surprises.

PRAYER: Lord, give me faith! — to live from day to day,
With tranquil heart to do my simple part,
And, with my hand in Thine, just go Thy way.

Lord, give me faith! — to trust, if not to know;
With quiet mind in all things Thee to find,
And child-like, go where Thou wouldst have me go.

Lord, give me faith! — to leave it all to Thee,
The future is Thy gift, I would not lift
The veil Thy love has hung twixt it and me.

(John Oxenham)

Take our thoughts and think through them; take our words and speak through them; and take our love and blend it with Christ's. Amen.

SEVEN CARDINAL VIRTUES: (6) HOPE

God wanted to make it very clear to those who were to receive what he promised that he would never change his purpose; so he added his vow to the promise. There are these two things, then, that cannot change and about which God cannot lie. So we who have found safety with him are greatly encouraged to hold firmly to the hope that is placed before us. We have this hope as an anchor for our hearts. It is safe and sure, and goes through the curtain of the heavenly temple into the inner sanctuary (Hebrews 6:17-19, TEV).

A painting by the Victorian artist and sculptor, George Frederic Watts, is entitled *Hope*. The picture shows a blindfolded woman sitting with bowed head. She is seated on a sphere or globe. The instrument she holds has only one string unbroken. In the dark sky, only one star shines. The artist puzzled some persons who do not think as easily as he did in symbols. Two London charwomen, sometimes euphemistically called "cleaning ladies," gazed at it once and were puzzled by it. *"Hope?"* said one, *"Hope?* Why is it called *Hope?"* To which the other replied, gazing at the figure perched precariously on the sphere, "I suppose because she hopes she won't fall off." The somewhat absurd story does represent what many people think of hope.

Too often, hope is thought of as an illusion, a will-o'-the-wisp that only a wishful thinker would chase. "What a hope!" we exclaim. One cynic said, "He that lives upon hope will die fasting."

Such despair is not the position of the New Testament. Whatever the ancient and medieval church made of cardinal virtues, the apostle Paul selected faith, hope, and love. He writes of the patience of hope, of the hope that "maketh not ashamed" (see Romans 5:5, KJV). As the Revised Standard Version gives it, "We rejoice in our hope of sharing the glory of God. . . . Character produces hope, and hope does not disappoint us, because God's love has been poured into our hearts through the Holy Spirit which has been given to us" (Romans 5:2, 4-5). As for the writer of the letter to Hebrew Christians, he declares that hope is "an anchor for our hearts . . . safe and sure." He then mixes or changes his metaphors and says that this anchor "goes through the curtain of the heavenly temple into the inner sanctuary" where Jesus has entered before us.

But to at least a few intelligent, decent men and women the urging to keep on hoping that the clouds will pass from the sky of their lives is a kind of mockery. To hope that something good may come where now there is so much that is disappointing, hurtful, evil, seems to be asking too much. "What is there to hope for," a so-called realist says to me, "in the midst of affluence, if you are poor? In the midst of family gatherings where you are alone? In the midst of love, where you feel rejected? What is there so hopeful for someone who sees the sparkling eyes of little children when he himself is trying devilishly hard to deal with his own childhood? When preachers talk about good news and hope, but you don't know where to turn for one reason or another, what is there to hope for?"

An observant Christian tourist offers this candid shot of something near despair: "I was visiting a little chapel one day, out in the Pacific Northwest. It was a small frame building with beautiful stained-glass windows. Because it was an Episcopal Church, it had a beautiful altar. When I left the church, I stopped to sign the guest register and I leafed through the pages to see if I recognized any of the names. There was one entry that caught my attention. No name was listed; just the date and these words, 'Thank you for a place to cry.'"

An authentic Christian church does not express chirpy optimism, any more than it emphasizes unrelieved despair. Christ's good news about God's love makes a place for the tears and then, as the last book of the Bible asserts, God wipes away every tear from the eyes of those who pour out to him their grief, frustration, heartbreak, and sense of keen loss. Jesus Christ was born in a violent world, as violent as our world today. He grew up in a tough world. He was the victim of greed, hatred, jealousy, and all the other evils of which men in any time are capable. But now we have hope, and we are saved by this hope.

A distinguished medical scientist associated with a famous university addressed a gathering of medical students. He reminded them that there are precious elements not easily examined by biochemical analysis, and he concluded by saying that one of the best tonics is hope. Of course there is a kind of optimism which may be compatible with a worsening condition, like that of some businessmen who persist in looking on the bright side of their accounts when they are about to wind up in trouble.

Those who confide themselves to Christ with a quiet and unquenchable hope are like a ship with an adequate anchor in a storm. Language which comes easily to the uncurable optimist is language which the believing Christian realist must discard. Why should we have a sure and steadfast hope? Here are some reasons that thoughtful, honest, and brave men and women have found to be valid.

We have hope that what should be shall be, because truth is indestructible. Lies do win early engagements. Indeed the truth we need to know to live as we should live may be nailed to a cross and taken down to be hidden in some tomb. But like the One who said, "I am the truth," truth itself will rise again. Somehow truth partakes of the life of God himself. Do you recall John Milton's words? "Let her (Truth) and Falsehood grapple; whoever knew Truth put to the worst in a free and open encounter. . . . For who knows not that Truth is strong next to the Almighty." You may also recall hearing these words by the late Sir Winston Churchill uttered in a dark time: "Truth is incontrovertible. Panic may resent it; ignorance may deride it; malice may distort it; but there it is."

Why can we hope, when hope seems gone? *Because God is on the throne.* The world is not meaningless, but God has created it for good. To hope in God means that we are persuaded that although God may not work our way, he works out his design. "So," to quote today's Scripture, "we who have found safety with him are greatly encouraged to hold firmly to the hope that is placed before us. We have this hope as an anchor for our hearts." God never violates any personality he has made. He seeks to win us, and change us and our world by all the inducements of his love. A man who worked in the midst of war and its devastation and cruelty wrote: "God seeks to win us to our hard task to have patience with the patience of God."

> Crowns and thrones may perish,
> Kingdoms rise and wane[1]

But God still rules in the affairs of men. We are either on the way with divine righteousness, goodness, and love, or we are in the way.

Why can we hope? Why should we hope? Why should we, in the midst of a turbulent, revolutionary world? Why should we hope when we confront a possible misfortune, long illness, a personal loss, or a humiliating defeat? *Because of the fact of Christ.* To the fact that on this ambiguous earth God's dealings and character have been told us, we must give him our faith, our trust. Faith and hope are inseparable. "By faith," says the New Testament, "you are saved through hope." Writing his first letter to his colleague Timothy, the apostle gave a wonderful description in two words of his Lord — and ours. "Paul, an apostle of Christ Jesus by command of God our Savior and of Christ Jesus, our hope" (1 Timothy 1:1). *"Christ Jesus, our hope."*

[1] Reprinted from "Onward Christian Soldiers." Used by permission of J. Curwin & Sons. Ltd.

Some years ago, the university where I worked gave me sabbatical leave and I taught at Westminster College, Cambridge, England. One of the joys of this tenure was occupying the house provided, despite the lack of central heating and some cold, damp days! It was next door to the home of two of the kindest persons I have ever known. The husband was the renowned Professor Herbert Henry Farmer. Some years before, I had heard him say something that had helped me much. Later published, here is the gist of it: Whenever he was confronted with moments of doubt and despair, one thing he always tried to do was to take another look at Jesus. What he saw, he said, was: "Not the somewhat meek and placid figure that looks down upon us from a stained glass window, or from the pictures in a book of Bible stories for children. . . . I see a being of literally tremendous intellectual power . . . above all, a being of intensest moral purity and strength, one so utterly released from himself that at one and the same time he has walked to the middle of the stage of history like a god, and yet has been forever afterwards the pattern of humility . . . as he is greater than I in every way, so he is more certain than I am of God. The fog of unbelief and doubt which drifts at times across my spirit is absent from his. I cannot but believe that his spirit saw the reality of things more clearly than mine. I cannot but ask myself the question again and again: Which, after all, are more likely to be right, the doubts of H. H. Farmer or the magnificent certainties of Jesus Christ? . . . It seems to me the sincere thing, to trust his certainties and that voice in my own soul which, however falteringly at times, point the same way." [2]

PRAYER: Christ, our Savior, come thou as love within us, that we go forth with the light of thy hope in our eyes, and thy faith and love in our hearts. Amen.

(from Gelasian Sacramentary)

[2] Herbert Henry Farmer, "Doubt and Faith" in G. P. Butler, *Best Sermons 1947-48* (New York: Harper & Row, Publishers, 1947), pp. 148-149.

Holy Spirit, instruct us with truth, inform us
with the good news of God's love, and enrich
us with the love of Christ. Amen.

SEVEN CARDINAL VIRTUES: (7) LOVE

*This is what love is: it is not that we have loved God, but that he
loved us and sent his Son to be the means by which our sins are
forgiven. Dear friends, if this is how God loved us, then we should
love one another (1 John 4:10-11, TEV).*

"This is what love is," says John. And we expect a definition. But we do not receive a verbal definition. How would
you define love, which Henry Drummond rightly said is "the
greatest thing in the world"? When we try to define "love,"
we are faced with the problem that the word has been
cheapened by sentimentality and lascivious connotations
which are all too common. Nevertheless, there is no other
word to replace it.

The crown of the cardinal virtues is love. And the writer
of First John catches our attention by saying, "God is love."
If we were not so blasé, so blunted, it would make us catch
our breath with its wonder. Two sentences later he excites
our curiosity by saying, "This is what love is: it is not that we
have loved God, but that he loved us and sent his Son to be
the means by which our sins are forgiven." But please, John,
we would appreciate having a clear, explicit definition.

Perhaps the best statement that can be put into words is

inadequate. Professor William Barclay has scriptural support for his definition. He has written that the fourth word for "love" which the Greeks invented — *agapé*, Christian love — is "unconquerable benevolence, invincible good will." Does that leave you cold? After all, a man does not say to his girl, the woman he adores, "My dear, I have unconquerable benevolence and invincible good will toward you. Will you marry me?" Of course not. Instead, the person who loves romantically and also "in depth" uses language, or tries to, such as Elizabeth Barrett used toward the man she loved and married, Robert Browning:

> How do I love thee? Let me count the ways.
> I love thee to the depth and breadth and height
> My soul can reach, when feeling out of sight
> For the ends of Being and ideal Grace.
> I love thee to the level of everyday's
> Most quiet need, by sun and candle-light. . . .
> I love thee with the breath,
> Smiles, tears, of all my life! — and, if God choose,
> I shall but love thee better after death.
>
> (From Sonnets from the Portuguese)

"This is what love is: it is not that we have loved God [with unconquerable benevolence], but that he loved us." We know God loves us because he "sent his Son to be the means by which our sins are forgiven," and that through Jesus Christ we might have life.

When God's love moves us to mutual love, there is one mark of creative love which we sometimes overlook. It is this: *Christian love loves enough to leave the one loved reasonably alone.* What does this mean? It does not mean that we isolate ourselves from the one loved. It certainly does not mean to leave the one loved to be lonely. Kahlil Gibran, the Eastern mystic, expressed it memorably: "Let there be spaces in your togetherness." True love includes reverence for the personality; it considers the rights and the needs of the other. It grants freedom for self-direction. The late C. S. Lewis, distinguished Cambrdige University scholar, tells of the opposite of such nonpossessive love in his book *The Four Loves*. He tells of an overactive and dominating mother, whom he calls Mrs. Fidget. "Mrs. Fidget very often said that she lived for her family. And it was not untrue. Everyone in the neighborhood knew it. 'She lives for her family,' they said; 'what a wife and mother!' She did all the washing; true, she did it badly, and they could have afforded to send it out to a laundry, and they frequently begged her not to do it. But she did. There was always a hot lunch for anyone who was at home and always a hot meal at night (even in midsummer). They implored her not to provide this. They protested almost with tears in their eyes (and with truth) that they liked cold meals. It made no difference. She was living for her family. She always sat up to 'welcome' you home if you were out late at night; two or three in the morning, it made no odds; you would always find the frail, pale, weary face awaiting you, like a silent accusation. Which meant of course that you couldn't with any decency go out very often. She was always making things too; being in her own estimation (I'm no judge myself) an excellent amateur dressmaker, and a great knitter. And of course, unless you were a heartless brute, you had to wear the things. (The Vicar tells me that, since her death, the contribution of that family alone to 'sales of work' [rummage sales] outweigh those of all his other parishioners put together.) . . . For Mrs. Fidget, as she so often said, would 'work her fingers to the bone' for her family. They couldn't stop her. Nor could they — being decent people — quite sit still and watch her do it. *They had to help.* Indeed they *were always having to help.* That is, they did things for her to help her to do things for them which they didn't want done."[1]

Do you and I love enough to leave the ones we love alone? To permit the loved person full freedom to be another person?

Here is encouragement for you. *Love can be learned.* Often human beings are tempted to consider love to be spurious. It seems like something put over on us. Or we think there is a special formula for experiencing the real thing. Love is not like falling into a heated swimming pool. It is something we grow into. Most human beings possess the power to give love and to receive love. When we fail in love, in evoking love

[1] C. S. Lewis, *The Four Loves* (Harcourt, Brace & World, Inc., 1960), pp. 74-75. Italics added.

from another person (and the love need not be romantic love), it is not because we have not the capacity, but because we have denied ourselves or been denied the experiences in which we grow into love and learn truly to love the other. The only advice needed here is the old wise saying: "Walk before you run." Learn to love yourself, to affirm yourself and then to affirm your friends. Only as we learn to love ourselves, to accept ourselves, and affirm ourselves, and then affirm, and accept, and love others — not just want them — that we can learn to love God. This learning to love ourselves, others, and God follows principles similar to learning on other levels. We must love each other before we can love God.

Jesus speaks of coming into God's presence, worshiping at an altar, and remembering your broken relationship with your brother or sister soul. He instructs us to cease our worship and give up our specifically religious exercise until we are reconciled to our estranged fellow human. Psychologist Eric Fromm, who gave us the helpful book *The Art of Loving*, asks us how can we love our neighbors whom we see only occasionally, until we have learned to love ourselves. Albert Schweitzer, physician in Africa, organist, theologian, and authority on Bach once visited the United States. At Aspen, Colorado, following an evening lecture, reporters quizzed him and pressed him to explain what he meant by "reverence for life." Finally he said, "All right, gentlemen, I will give you just one more illustration of what I mean by 'reverence for life.' As of this minute, we are going to start reverencing my life. You are going home, and I am going to bed!"

You and I can learn to love by loving ourselves as Christ taught and demonstrated, by loving others with something of Christ's grace, and by loving God with all our lives.

As we think of this basic matter, consider one more insight that has helped to kindle "steadfast love" for many! *Love wins even when it loses.* Someone put it this way: love wins more when it loses than hate knows when it wins! Jesus died in agony on the cross. At that moment, if anyone had evaluated that death as a victory would he not have been considered insane? But we do so assess it. We sing, "In the cross of Christ I glory, towering o'er the wrecks of time."

Too commonly we confuse the power to win with the power genuinely to succeed. Here is a young couple with power to get married. After a few weeks or months of married life they discover they need another kind of power — the power to succeed in a loving, understanding, mutually forgiving relationship. Likewise, in other matters we may have power to win the particular world we covet and yet lose our own souls. Our Lord had to recognize that his love, God's love, cannot always produce the immediate or even fairly long-term results he expected. But he learned and demonstrated that love remains love, and love remains alive. Life can crucify the best God can offer, but love has power to endure and to transmute defeat into victory.

It all adds up to this: the four-letter word for God is *love*. "This is what love is: it is not that we have loved God, but that he loved us and sent his Son to be the means by which our sins are forgiven. Dear friends, if this is how God loved us, then we should love one another."

PRAYER: Open our lives to thy love, O God, by enabling us to risk our security and peace of mind through loving others as Christ loved. For thy love's sake, and ours. Amen.

Blessed Lord, show thyself alive to us by the warming of our hearts and the knowing of thy truth in our minds. Amen.

HOW CHRIST CONQUERS DEATH

We know that Christ being raised from the dead will never die again; death no longer has dominion over him (Romans 6:9).

We can be sure that the risen Christ never dies again — death's power to touch him is finished (Phillips).

Imagine, if you can, this happening. You come to church today — this church, any Christian church. The doors are locked. On every door is a printed sign with the startling legend:

Closed until further notice.

Underneath that large headline is this statement: "Yesterday incontrovertible evidence was presented to leaders and representatives of all churches, Eastern Orthodox, Protestant, Roman Catholic, that the resurrection of Jesus of Nazareth never occurred. His grave has been located and in it with his remains is documentary proof that his first followers had secretly removed his body from the garden tomb once owned by a certain Joseph of Arimathea. With profound sorrow the heads of all the churches and church councils acknowledge that the foundation belief of Christianity for nineteen centuries has now been proved false. A special council may be convened in Geneva or Rome to determine what shall be the future position of the Christian church. Please wait patiently for further news which will be reported over the news media."

What if the Resurrection faith is a gigantic hoax? Of course, there are many who disbelieve the Easter story now, and in every era since the first Easter morning there have been unbelievers. For millions of Christians however, the consequences of such a disclosure would be disastrous. There would be a kind of epidemic of despair. Of all men we would be the most miserable. Shaken would be the confidence that truth ultimately triumphs over falsehood; that goodness, not evil, will win; that love, not hate, has the future with it; that God lives and "keepeth watch above his own." The highest in human nature would be at the mercy of the lowest; physical death would mean spiritual death. Many would feel their own minds and spirits enveloped by a cosmic chill of utter loneliness. The great unseen Companion and Friend would be dead forever. In the ringing affirmation of Robert Browning,

> "But Easter-Day breaks! But Christ rises!
> Mercy every way is infinite. . . ."

The trumpets keep sounding what the Apostle Paul wrote to the Church in Rome: "We know that Christ being raised from the dead will never die again; death no longer has dominion over him." Let J. B. Phillips translate the same affirmation: "We can be sure that the risen Christ never dies again — death's power to touch him is finished."

Death's power to touch him was real power. The New Testament, the Scriptures produced by the young church, testify to that. "Christ died for our sins." But he died. It was not a case of fainting and being secretly revived by his close friends. Roman officials were careful to make sure that a man who had been sentenced to death was indisputably dead when he was interred in a grave or tomb. But now "death's power to touch him is finished." This is not merely to say that Christ lives in the memory of those who loved him. It is infinitely more than saying that death cannot touch Christ now because he has an immortality of influence. "Christ being raised from the dead will never die again."

Easter is God's victory day. We celebrate the risen Lord's reality because the risen Lord abides. Good Friday without Easter leaves a huge question mark against the sky of life. The cross does not stand alone. Easter is truly the interpretation of Good Friday. The resurrection of Christ is God's act of making known, by the supreme miracle, the victory of God's saving purpose which took Christ to the cross. Wrote Professor Archibald M. Hunter, "We do well to fix our gaze on Calvary; but we never see it aright until we see it with the light of the first Easter morning breaking behind that Cross upon the lonely hill." [1]

"Christ being raised from the dead dieth no more; death hath no more dominion over him" (KJV).

How does Christ conquer death? How does he conquer every kind of death?

First, *Christ demonstrates the resurrection fact.* But is it a fact of the kind which scientifically trained men and women can test? No, it is not a fact in the precise technical sense. But some of the most trustworthy minds have sifted all the evidence and declare that the evidence is to be trusted. The earliest evidence in the fifteenth chapter of First Corinthians goes back to within a few years of the event itself. It goes back to a time where there were literally hundreds still living who, with their own eyes, had seen Christ risen and alive. Paul virtually says: "If you won't take my word for it, ask them. They saw him after death and the event completely changed their lives."

When all tests have been applied, two things emerge unshaken. First, Joseph of Arimathea's rock-tomb lost its tenant. Second, Christ appeared alive to many people and talked with them. You can find other explanations of these two facts. Think also of the silence of Christ's enemies. They regarded Christ as an imposter who deserved the death he received. Yet within a few days of his death the wildest rumors were going. Why didn't his enemies show that these rumors were false? Because they could not. Then look at the great change in the characters and personalities of his first followers. Only

[1] Archibald M. Hunter, *Teaching and Preaching the New Testament* (London: SCM Press, Ltd., 1963), p. 105.

the Resurrection will explain why men who at Calvary "forsook him and fled" a week later were ready to take on the whole world unafraid. Then what are we to make of the evidence of the church itself? Never let us forget that the resurrection of Jesus Christ from the dead is the foundation of the church. If he had died but a martyr's death, they would have remembered him for a time, but after that his life and actions would have been known to only a few research students. Yet, it is true that only the Resurrection can explain the existence and the persistence of the holy, universal church.

There is more. Christ's victory over death and evil is *attested by Christ making himself known as alive in and among his own.* Many believe that when Christ rose from the dead he assumed a different mode of existence. His spiritual body showed continuity with the body of flesh and blood which he had before death. But now he was operating in a new vehicle or body. Christ became more real to his followers than ever before. Closed doors could not withstand him. Armed guards could not hold him. Death's power to touch him was finished.

Nor was this experience of the risen and living Lord confined only to the first Christians. It has been experienced again and again in history. Samuel Rutherford in the seventeenth century, thrown into jail because of his Christian witness, wrote in his diary: "Jesus Christ came to me in my cell last night." Three centuries later, Charles Raven records a similar encounter in an English city slum. "Christ is alive, as alive as I am myself," sings Dr. R. W. Dale in Birmingham, while Albert Schweitzer, a twentieth-century Christian hero, wrote: "He comes to us as of old he came to them by the lakeside; and he speaks to us the same word, 'Follow me.' " John Greenleaf Whittier quietly added his personal testimony: "But warm, sweet, tender, even yet a present help is He; and faith has still its Olivet and love its Galilee." Because of this hope Christians are confident that what should be shall be. Efforts to abolish war will win; efforts to build a strong, united, just America will win.

> Shakespeare is dust, and will not come
> To question from his Avon tomb,

And Socrates and Shelley keep
An Attic and Italian sleep. . . .

They see not. But, O Christians, who
Throng Holborn and Fifth Avenue,
May you not meet, in spite of death,
A traveler from Nazareth?[2]

Once more, *Christ conquers the power of death by giving us a deathless hope.* Christ does not promise automatic immortality for everyone. Indeed eternal life — resurrection — is for all who put their confidence in him. When a man or woman, or a company of men and women and children are "in Christ" they may be sure that they will be *with* Christ forever. We do not go automatically to heaven. When we use the faith God gives us and the love he inspires we may be made one with him and thus hope to defeat the last enemy and to share Christ's eternal life.

We know very little about the next dimension of life! But isn't it enough that it is our Father's house, a place prepared for a people? Think of how reluctant an unborn baby would be if he could know that at birth he will be in a different kind of world than he had known. It will be a world of air, but unborn he lives without air. It will be a world with light, but unborn he lives without light. How can he live with such weird elements and conditions? But when the newborn child becomes aware of anything, he knows that strong loving hands are around him, and eyes full of love and tenderness are looking into his own. He had been prepared for this new life, this new environment. All unknown to him, he had been developing eyes for light which he had never yet seen, ears for sounds which he had never yet heard, lungs for air which he had never yet breathed. As one has said, "If God so carefully guards our entry into this world, will he be so careless about our entry into the next?" "Do not be worried and upset," Jesus told them. "Believe in God, and believe also in me. . . . I will come back and take you to myself, so that you will be where I am" (John 14:1, 3, TEV).

[2] From "To and Fro About the City" by John Drinkwater in *Masterpieces of Religious Verse,* edited by James D. Morrison (New York: Harper & Row, Publishers, 1948), p. 260, No. 812.

A five-year-old boy was on his first ride on a transcontinental railroad. When the train plunged into the first tunnel and blackness enfolded all, he gasped. Suddenly the train cleared the tunnel and daylight took over. The boy exclaimed, "It is tomorrow today!" In Jesus Christ we have found it to be true. It is tomorrow today!

"We know that Christ being raised from the dead will never die again"; death's power to touch him and those united with him is finished.

PRAYER: O risen Lord, surprise us with thy presence and thy joy. Make this church and every church truly a community of the resurrection, for thy love's sake. Amen.

Be thou God to us now, not in our way but in thy way, through Jesus Christ our Lord. Amen.

DEAR GOD, WHERE ARE YOU?

My tears have become my bread, by night, by day, as I hear it said all the day long: "Where is your God?" (Psalm 42:3, Gelineau translation).

If you or I do not see or hear any bad news, it is probably because we haven't been looking or listening! For the world is full of what are now called "hangups." A perceptive Christian woman wrote of this condition clearly: "As we read the newspaper or listen to the news by radio or television, who is there who has not occasionally remarked, 'I wish they would tell us good news once in awhile!' To be sure, the vocation of newscasters is to tell us the unusual, and the fact that so much is unmentioned as life moves on in a relatively even tenor in many thousands of homes and communities is a silent tribute to the fact that not all is wrong in our world . . . there is plenty of bad news. The war in Vietnam as it drags on its tragic, death-dealing way; the unsolved problems of the Middle East and many tensions elsewhere; a rising crime rate; a steadily increasing divorce rate and slipping sexual standards; increasing addiction to alcohol and drugs; death on the highways and in the air and from riots that destroy both life and property; murder and suicide at every level of society — these are among the things that fill the news."[1]

You could add to the list of woes and hangups. There is the unexplained evil which strikes our planet from time to time. Insurance policies speak of such events, ironically, as "acts of God." Then we could cite the general anxiety, loneliness, depression, and frustrations of many people. It makes you think of the somewhat humorous response made by a tenor soloist in a church I once served. My younger colleague in the church was temperamentally inclined to pessimism. In my absence, he preached on the man with the plumbline featured in the Book of Amos. From this passage he analyzed the dreadful plight of human beings and human society. Unfortunately he did not leave sufficient time to report the Christian cure. He left the congregation hanging over the abyss of doom. The tenor soloist was overheard whispering to the baritone soloist, "Can you lend me a rope or a gun?" If the bad news is all there is, why go on?

I cannot give you, and will not attempt to give you, a neatly packaged answer to the sharp questions which I have focused in one question, "Dear God, where are you?" If God exists, and if God is a loving as well as a holy and righteous heavenly Father, the God and Father of the Lord Jesus Christ, where is he when so much seems senseless, devilish, and irrational?

One fact is not debatable. This question is not new. It has been asked again and again by honest, realistic men and women. Repeatedly in the Bible you will find similar questions. "Why dost thou hide thy face?" (Psalm 88:14). "Why . . . art [thou] silent when the wicked swallows up a man more righteous than he?" (Habakkuk 1:13). Then look at Psalm 42. In the recent translation by a French scholar the author writes almost pathetically,

> Like the deer that yearns
> for running streams,
> so my soul is yearning
> for you, My God. . . .

---

[1] Georgia Harkness, *Stability Amid Change* (Nashville: Abingdon Press, 1969), p. 13.

when can I enter and see
the face of God?

My tears have become my bread,
by night, by day,
as I hear it said all the day long:
"Where is your God?" [2]

My purpose today is not to get you just to forget the dark side of life and look at the bright side. It is to point out that the universe, our world, and your lives are alive and alight with God's presence.

One true answer to the question, "Dear God, where are you?" of course is, *God is everywhere.* Let us be more specific, even if being specific still keeps us in the area of great generalizations.

First, *God's presence and power may be discerned in the dependable, unfailing order of his creation.* God cannot be dislodged. His reality imparts an eternal steadiness to this unimaginably vast universe. Our astronauts were not blind to God's reality when they soared where no human being had ever traveled previously. Werner von Braun, the world-renowned scientist, said to an interviewer at Cape Kennedy recently: "We must learn to consider God as Creator of the Universe and Master of everything. We need a greater Lord than we have had in the past!" . . . "Our outlook through the peephole at the vast universe only confirms our belief in the certainty of its Creator." [3] I had a friend who wistfully remarked that he wished God had a public relations department! He said he wished that God would advertise more. Several Madison Avenue ideas suggest themselves. "This tree comes through the courtesy of the Almighty." "This sunset is the gift of the eternal God." "This star, this planet, is kept in orbit through the wisdom and generous provision of a divine Benefactor." At Cape Kennedy a little boy was about to say his bedtime prayer. He was keenly aware of all the missile shots. In his prayer he said, "I hope they don't kill God!" My young friend, there's not much danger. The di-

[2] Joseph Gelineau, *The Psalms, A New Translation* (Philadelphia: the Westminster Press, 1963), p. 76.
[3] *Miami Herald,* June 21, 1969.

vine order, which is so important to scientists and astronauts, is not likely to be destroyed. "Dear God, where are you?" Out there. Down here. Everywhere.

Dear God, where are you? *In the moral order.* God's presence and will are operating in what is called the inexorable law of judgment. God is not an overindulgent grandparent. The moral law is not falling apart. Rather, what is falling apart are the ideas we often try to live by. Someone has wisely said: "God does not pay at the end of every week, but at the end he pays." Tyrants and gangsters, the cruel and the greedy, still overreach themselves. They dig their own inglorious graves. The gospel is not all a message of doom. A cartoon once showed the angel Gabriel about to blow his horn to close the whole show on our planet. The Almighty is shown looking down on the earth and he says to his executive officer, "Hold it, Gabriel. They're going to have another summit conference." God is in the midst of all the conflicts, the clashing forces, and he is in every attempt to end violence, injustice, and terror.

God is in the world he has made and is making and he is striving, with our cooperation, to move us upward from the jungle to the kingdom of Heaven on earth. In World War I, during a lull in trench warfare, a young soldier was talking with his commander. "Captain," said the younger man, "where is God?" At that moment two stretcher-bearers climbed over the top and moved under enemy fire to pick up a wounded soldier groaning in his pain. The captain said, "Look, son, there he is. There goes God now." God is involved. He is no imperturbable spectator of the human drama. He is in every deed of compassion, in every measure of forgiveness, in every social crisis, in every hospital, in every United Fund Drive, and in our churches when they are concerned with obeying the Savior's great commission to go into the world to feed the hungry, heal the sick, teach the ignorant, right wrongs, and proclaim the good news of Jesus Christ.

"Dear God, where are you?" *God is in your own soul.* As the Bible affirms,

> "The Lord is near to the brokenhearted,
> and saves the crushed in spirit" (Psalm 34:18).

The influential Christian thinker, Paul Tillich, emphasized strongly that God is wherever there is depth in any life. We are conscious of depth not only when we have done wrong. We have known the deeps when we have been moved by great music, poetry, drama, or some other form of true art. Deep calls to deep, in genuine love. Life had depth when you looked down at the sleeping form of your first child, or when you had to face the reality of death. We are conscious frequently that deep calls unto deep. God is in that depth.

When you look at men and women who are like little Christs to others, you know where God is. God clothes himself with surrendered personalities. In every age God has been found in such people.

"Dear God, where are you?" *God is to be experienced in Jesus Christ.* Jesus was no accidental by-product of a chance collocation of atoms. Perhaps you saw the comedy show on television known as "Laugh-In" when Dr. Billy Graham was the featured participant. He had some delightful one-sentence quips. However, at the end Rowan and Martin, the show's principal actors, became serious. They said to him, "Dr. Graham, we understand that a majority of those who attend your meetings are under twenty-five years of age. We would like to know how you do it; what is your message that brings them and apparently reaches many of them?" Billy Graham acknowledged that a surprisingly large percentage of the people in his audiences were young people. He then said, "I have the message I believe they most want to hear. It is this: 'God so loved the world, that he gave his only begotten Son, that whosoever believeth in him should not perish, but have everlasting life.'" Arte Johnson, who plays a German soldier, was then shown saying, "Very interesting . . . and very true." And then he added: "Think about it." When we ask, "Where is thy God?" we answer: "In Jesus Christ, crucified, risen, and living . . . the Word . . . God himself, made flesh to dwell among us."

Where is God? He is in his orderly, marvelous creation, in the moral order, in you and other dedicated men and women, in the depths of life, in Jesus Christ, and in his body, the church.

PRAYER: Dear God, thou art in all and through all and over all. We are especially grateful that thou hast come near to us in Jesus Christ, whose presence we may experience at any time, in any place. Amen.

Holy Spirit, speak to us as we speak and listen,
that we may live for God the life we ought to
live. Through Christ our Lord. Amen.

DON'T LOOK NOW,
BUT WE'RE BEING FOLLOWED!

*Surely goodness and mercy [kindness] shall follow me all the days of
my life (Psalm 23:6).*

"Don't look now, but we're being followed." These words
sound like a line from a James Bond thriller, or from "Mission
Impossible." However, we will consider them not as a warn-
ing to be alert to enemies, but as an exciting call to release
certain ennobling emotions, such as appreciation of all those
who have preceded us and all those who run the race of life
with us; and gratitude for God's blessings, past, present, and
future.

A highly respected and distinguished Christian leader in
our time, and one of the most popular preachers of the last
forty years, was Dr. Ralph W. Sockman, minister emeritus
of Christ United Methodist Church, New York City. One of
his favorite illustrations came from an episode he witnessed
in the 1948 Olympics. "Just in front of the grandstand where
he was seated, the second and third runners in the relay races
exchanged batons. The French team in one race had built
up an early lead. The first two runners had started fast and
had moved out ahead of the other teams. But just as the third

runner on the French team was taking the baton — he dropped it. This obviously put his team out of the race. So distressed was the responsible runner that he fell to the ground, put his hands over his head, and wept bitterly and openly. He was still showing great anguish as he was led from the stadium."

Dr. Sockman commented: "To take defeat so tearfully might seem a bit unsportsmanlike, were it not remembered how many persons were involved in that runner's failure. There were his watching compatriots with their crushed hopes. There were the teammates who had run before him and whose work was now ruined. And there was the runner who was to come after, but who now would never get a chance to run at all."

Life, says Paul, is a relay race. "I press on," he said in a famous passage, "I press on toward the goal for the prize of the upward call of God in Christ Jesus" (Philippians 3:14). Life's relay is something we did not initiate, and we shall not finish it. But we do run in it, even if our present condition hardly qualifies us to run in an actual Olympics contest!

Of course much depends on our stamina and our fitness, and much depends on our teammates. But how we individually perform is also of urgent importance. The New Testament uses the same figure of speech, and asks in the opening verses of the twelfth chapter of the letter to the Hebrew Christians: "And what of ourselves? With all these witnesses to faith around us like a cloud, we must throw off every encumbrance, every sin to which we cling [every clinging sin], and run with resolution [patience, perseverance] the race for which we are entered, our eyes fixed on Jesus, on whom faith depends from start to finish: Jesus who, for the sake of the joy that lay ahead of him, endured the cross, making light of its disgrace, and has taken his seat at the right hand of the throne of God" (Hebrews 12:1-2, NEB).

First, *we are being followed by those who have gone before us.* We follow them, to be sure. But in a spiritual sense they follow us. These are the "cloud of witnesses." Do we forget them? What of the men and women who helped us on our way? What of the church members and the others who befriended us, perhaps when we felt we were complete failures?

We need to remember the words of Mark Hopkins, the famous educator who was president of Williams College a hundred years ago. A student who was the son a wealthy patron of the institution quite flippantly offered to pay for some damage which he had caused in the village. Speaking about the incident, Mark Hopkins said, "Rich young men come here and take that tone as if they could pay for what they get here. No student can pay for what he gets at Williams College. Who can pay for the sacrifices of Colonel Williams and all other benefactors? Every man here is a charity student!"

Aren't we all? Does any student pay more than 80 percent of what it actually costs in money to keep him in school? Can any of us who worship here really pay for what we receive? Can you pay for the prophets, apostles, saints, martyrs, St. Francis of Assisi, Martin Luther, the Wesleys, John Calvin, John Knox, John Robinson of Pilgrim Fathers' fame, and the pastoral care and exposition of the Word provided by the faithful men and women we knew in our childhood, youth, and adult years? Can you pay for Christ on the cross? Without fear of jingoistic flag waving, what about our heritage? Can anyone really pay for Valley Forge, or for Gettysburg? For the men who died at Chateau-Thierry and the Somme in World War I; on Bataan, in Normandy, at Salerno, and in Africa and Italy in World War II to prevent insanity from ruling the free world? For Korea and Vietnam? For our Constitution built out of stress? Surely we can be grateful for all of these. And we can live appreciatively. We can carry the baton that is handed to us. Don't look now, but we're being followed! Yes, says the poet who gave us our best-loved psalm: "Goodness and mercy shall follow me all the days of my life." Look now! We're being followed by our real creditors.

We are being followed, observed, and counted upon by those who ran the race before we ever arrived. *We are also being followed by those who come after us.* At the three hundredth anniversary of Harvard University the freshman class carried a streetwide banner. On it they had inscribed the words: "This University waited 300 years for us!" Well, conceited as it sounded, it was true. This sentiment should evoke gratitude as well as call forth responsibility. There is a sense in which every local church has waited nineteen hundred years for the new members who unite with it. The edifice and the fellowship and the program we have received, and these are what we may bequeath not only intact but enlarged, enlivened, and enriched by our faithfulness, love, and service. Don't throw them lightly away. Marshall McLuhan, the author of *The Medium Is the Massage* (or the Medium Is the Message), vows that he saw on a billboard in Toronto, Canada, this sign: "Help beautify our junkyards — throw something lovely away!" This may be part of the evangelism of ecology! The gospel of Christ, the Christian ethic and morality, and the integrity Christians are asked to build into themselves and their community are among the lovely things we can throw away by negligence, niggardliness, and carelessness. Don't try to beautify the junkyard of history by throwing lovely things into it!

Don't look now, but we're being followed. *We are being followed by the divine Love and Justice, God himself.* The only known way of keeping faith with those who have gone before, those who come after us, the under-thirty crowd, the boys and girls, and the children yet unborn is to relate ourselves vitally to the Source without whom we could not have begun, and without whose energizing power we could not have run the race thus far. Francis Thompson called God "the Hound of Heaven." God pursues us, and we cannot escape his love, power, wisdom, and truth. He seeks us. In every letter we write, every conversation we have, every breath we draw, every dollar we spend, and every love we share, God confronts us. Although many divine-human encounters go unnoticed by us, God is surely present in them. He is active, initiating, continuing, and concluding.

This is what the psalmist affirmed when he said, "Surely goodness and mercy shall follow me all the days of my life." To speak of a shepherd is to think of a shepherd's dogs. Even today, with modern vehicles and improved methods of caring for sheep and lambs, sheep dogs are essential. The astonishing thing to me is the sheep dog's loyalty and honor. He will finish the day exhausted and with bleeding feet, but with not a single sheep lost. An old preacher fastened on this thought: "'The Lord is my shepherd,' he cried, 'aye, and more than that, he has two fine collie dogs, Goodness and Mercy. With him before and them behind, even poor sinners like you and me can hope to win home at last.'"[1]

Look now! Someone is following us! Because of this divine Pursuer we take courage and thank God. You will, won't you? Thank God that his goodness and mercy follow us all the days of our lives and that we shall dwell in the house of the Lord forever.

PRAYER: Lord, when we recall a little of all thou hast done and art doing for us, we cannot take life for granted but for gratitude. With the psalmist of old we say, "Bless the Lord, O my soul, and forget not all his benefits." In Christ. Amen.

[1] J. R. P. Sclater in *The Interpreter's Bible* (Nashville: Abingdon Press, 1956), vol. 4, p. 130.

Enable us, O Holy Spirit, to receive thy light,
that in any darkness we may rise into confidence
and courage. Through Christ. Amen.

WHY MUST GOD'S CHILDREN SUFFER?

The wound which is borne in God's way brings a change of heart too salutary to regret; but the hurt which is borne in the world's way brings death. You bore your hurt in God's way, and see what its results have been! (2 Corinthians 7:10-11, NEB).

Why must God's children suffer? This is one of the hardest questions for Christians to face. Neither I nor any other Christian has a wholly adequate answer. True, the non-Christian, particularly the atheist, has a problem connected with suffering. He may accept evil as an inescapable part of meaningless existence but he has to face the problem of good. What is the source of so much that is good in life, such as sacrificial love and unselfish deeds? But the believer in the God of holy, righteous love must also ask about evil in all its sharpness. For since Jesus is the Christ, God's unique revelation, then God is holy, righteous love. And if God is love, how can he possibly send suffering to his children who trust him and try to live as responsible members of his family?

To this question, I am sure the answer is, bluntly, *God does not send suffering or pain.* God's perfect will, his ideal intention, is the perfect health — physical, mental, and spiritual — of all of his children. Jesus taught that sickness is the work of Satan. When a woman who had been ill for eighteen years was brought to Jesus, he healed her. He did not say that her illness was the will of God. Most explicitly he described her as "this woman, a daughter of Abraham whom Satan bound for eighteen years" (Luke 13:16). The apostle Paul speaks of the thorn or stake in his flesh as "a messenger of Satan, to harass me" (2 Corinthians 12:7). You may regard the name "Satan" as a "powerful evil intelligence" or as a symbol for the evil which happens to us from the mass ignorance, folly and sin of mankind. As Dr. Leslie D. Weatherhead has written, how we think of Satan in this connection does not affect the question. "Any pain worth calling 'suffering' is evil. It is something that ought not to be." [1]

But does not God allow suffering? The answer must be yes. The explanation of why a loving and almighty God allows suffering is not wholly clear. But as able Christian thinkers remind us, like the best of human parents, our heavenly Father allows what he does not will. If he did not allow us to do wrong and did not allow us to "suffer the slings and arrows of outrageous fortune" which include physical disease and crippling accidents, human beings would have no free will, no freedom of choice. Here is a little boy or girl learning to walk. When the child takes his first steps, he is likely to stumble and fall. We hope his first attempts are on a soft carpet. You certainly do not will him or intend him to fall, or else you would push him over. He is learning to walk and you try to provide the best conditions. If he wanted to do his learning on a railway bridge where trains are likely to come, you certainly would not permit him to walk or fall there. Could it be otherwise with God and his children? God wants us to learn the laws of health and life, to overcome our ignorance, and to turn away from sin. This may well be the reason the God of love allows suffering.

When we think of the suffering of good folks — men, women, and children — we confront a mystery. But those who believe in the nature of God as Jesus taught and disclosed it are convinced that God is love. So we must say that God allows

[1] Leslie D. Weatherhead, *Salute to a Sufferer* (London: Epworth Press, 1962), p. 12.

the evil of suffering to afflict his children. But in saying this we must quickly add what someone calls "a hidden treasure for us which is worth picking up." It is this: *If He allows it, it means He can use it for our good."* [2]

Now join me in moving further into elements in the Christian answer to this question. We have affirmed our belief that God is holy, righteous love; that each one of us his children is loved by God. This means, too, that God is working out his own purpose in each of our lives. We have also said, on the strength of the Bible and particularly the word of our Lord, that God does not intend that any of his children should suffer. Christ devoted much of his energy and life to fighting disease and curing illness. God allows it in this developing world which means that, while he does not will it, he can use it ultimately for something precious to weave into his perfect pattern.

What more can we say with honesty and humility?

Much of the suffering endured by good persons, by Christians as well as sincerely religious persons of other faiths, is mysterious. In a long life no one escapes some form of loss, disability, or illness. It is foolish to torture ourselves by asking "What have I done to deserve this?" Much of what happens to us seems to be part of the price we pay for belonging to the human family. Because of belonging to the human family we gain much that we do not earn or deserve, just as we experience much that is evil which is not related to our own personal ignorance, folly, or sin. What sometimes happens to us — an accident, for example — has no personal connection with our own sin or ignorance or foolishness. When you watch a football player thrown by an opponent, and sometimes hurt (especially if he is a formidable quarterback) you never hear him lie down and say, "Why should this happen to me?"

Here is a second insight that has helped many. *Suffering is sometimes punitive.* A Lutheran pastor, Dr. Wallace E. Fisher, expressed it, "The gospel enables us to accept the awful truth [that some] suffering is . . . the consequence of man's abuse of his freedom." Jesus said bluntly, "What a man sows, he also reaps." This is true whether what we sow is good or

[2] *Ibid.,* p. 17.

evil. Mental anguish can sometimes be traced to a loose tongue, spreading cruel gossip or cruel criticism. Some physical suffering, such as some malignancies, are traceable to over-indulgence in some habit. If I am a cigarette smoker and the doctor advises me to quit but I do not, am I not punishing myself? I cannot blame God or anyone else if I develop some dangerous disease as the result of smoking. Spiritual suffering may be caused by unconfessed sin which leads to unrelieved guilt. Yes, says the pastor, "Wave after wave rolls in as un-disciplined lives collide with physical and moral laws of God's universe." [3] Moreover, we may be punished because we are involved in an entire community's sin. Guilt is frequently corporate. Says the Bible, "all we like sheep have gone astray." No man is an island, John Donne said long ago. We are interrelated.

Christ also teaches that suffering may be remedial. The drama of the Book of Job is the classic treatment of this idea. Parents often feel agony when their children suffer, but parents who care deeply for their children sometimes must exercise painful discipline. They do not apply this discipline in anger, vindictiveness, or hard feelings, but they do it know-ing that no human being ever develops into someone more mature without a measure of suffering. A surgeon's operation may produce suffering, even with the use of modern drugs, but a good surgeon may be Christ's own helper and God's healing agent. Our New Testament declares that even the Son of God, Jesus Christ himself, "although he was a Son, he learned obedience through what he suffered" (Hebrews 5:8).

Suffering, allowed by God, although not the perfect will of God, can be so accepted that it becomes redemptive. Jesus laid it on the line: we can inherit the abundant life, possess the divine kingdom, only as we take up our cross and follow him into the world and on to Calvary. What is it to bear the cross? It is to accept voluntary suffering for Christ's sake. When we accept unavoidable suffering and offer it to the Lord, Christ himself joins us. He not only sympathizes, he enters into our suffering. He is a participant. Now we come

[3] Wallace E. Fisher, *Preaching and Parish Renewal* (Nashville: Abing-don Press, 1966), pp. 61ff.

to the great biblical word of Paul in 2 Corinthians 7:10. The old version was "godly sorrow worketh repentance to salvation not to be repented of" (KJV). Dr. Moffatt speaks of "godly sorrow" as "the pain God is allowed to guide." The *New English Bible* translates it, "the wound which is borne in God's way." When you and I are in the midst of our suffering — be it mental, physical, or spiritual — it is hard to see God's presence and purpose in it. But when we look back, we feel that there was "A Hand that guided and a Hand that planned."

I would like to speak as tenderly and as honestly as I know how, to anyone who experiences the frustration and loneliness or the discouragement of weakness or pain. God wants you to have life, as Jesus said, "in all its fullness" (John 10:10, NEB). One great Christian soul used to say "It is not wicked to be ill, but it is wicked to be more ill than you need to be." God provides many resources with which to fight illness. One is the competent physician or the skillful surgeon. Others are therapists of different kinds, such as psychiatrists, physiotherapists, and efficient, conscientious nurses. Still other aids come from technological sources. But let us not discount the power of Christian faith and prayer. Prayer is a means of letting God's healing Spirit do his tremendous work. Often an instructed minister or Christian layman whom we trust can help us to think out the relationship of religion to our suffering. We may need to see that our Christian life is in good order. Who does not know how the bottling up of fear, anxiety, hate, resentment, malice, or guilt can set off an illness and delay its recovery? Doctors are increasingly aware of this. Prayer for healing is an immensely powerful force. For such prayer at its best aims to bring the patient into as complete a unity with God as is possible. Faith is more than believing certain propositions. It is trust. As someone has said, "Faith, then, is quietly trusting the God who is like Jesus [who is in Jesus] whether one is healed or not, knowing that we are safe, that God loves us, is at work in us and through us, and will use the suffering if, for various reasons, it cannot yet be ended." You and I can have that kind of faith by looking to him, by talking with him, by listening, and by loving. This is how to bear the wound, the hurt, in God's way. One day the Lord Himself may say to you: *"You bore your hurt in God's way and see what its results have been!"*

PRAYER: O God to whom all thy children are dear, assure us that thy glorious purpose can never be defeated, that nothing can ever snatch us from thy loving care, in Jesus Christ our Savior and Lord. Amen.

NOT THE END BUT A BEND IN THE ROAD

*I will lead the blind
  in a way that they know not,
in paths that they have not known
  I will guide them.
I will turn the darkness before them into light,
  the rough places into level ground.
These are the things I will do,
  and I will not forsake them (Isaiah 42:16).*

A teacher in a church school asked her class, "What is a prophet?" There was a long silence. Then a fairly young boy said timidly: "It's a man who gets to know what God's thinking." When you read any of the passages in chapters forty through fifty-five of the Book of Isaiah, you should be convinced that the author had gotten to know what God was thinking. The writer of these chapters is sometimes named the Second Isaiah. He may have been the disciple of the Isaiah of Jerusalem who gave us chapters 1 through 39. Why are many scholars convinced that chapters 40 through 55 are the work of a disciple of the Isaiah of chapters 1 to 39? Because of the very different literary style. Also, his world is different from the one in which the first Isaiah lived and

116

wrote. "Judah has ceased to exist; Jerusalem is in ruins; Assyria has been replaced as the world empire by Babylon and Babylon itself is on the point of being supplanted by the new power of Persia under its remarkable ruler Cyrus. The scene is the Exile, the audience is the sometimes despondent, sometimes hopeful Jewish community in Babylon. . . ."[1] These people were separated by many miles of desert country from the places they called home. Some of their spiritual leaders had tried to persuade them that the Exile was a necessary discipline, a time for some deep thinking and some radical changes in their way of living. You may be sure that many could not accept that lofty view, but instead felt that the Almighty had deserted them. Many were near to tears when they recalled the life and the persons they once knew and enjoyed. They needed a message of comfort and words of hope. This is what the prophet whom we call Second Isaiah provided:

> "Console my people, console
>   them —
> 'tis the voice of your God —
> speak to Jerusalem tenderly,
>   proclaim to her
> that her hard days are ended,
>   her guilt paid off" (Moffatt).

These are the opening words of chapter 40 and they sound the note which dominates the writer's work.

Do we need this message from God today? We have not been deported. Most of us are not suffering from poverty, at least from the economic kind. But we may be exiled from deep peace and valid hope. So we turn to the prophet Isaiah's words in the forty-second chapter of Isaiah. He has learned what God is thinking and he hears the Eternal saying,

> I will lead the blind
>   in a way that they know not,
> in paths that they have not known
>   I will guide them.

[1] William Neil, *Harper's Bible Commentary* (New York: Harper & Row, Publishers. Copyright © 1962 by Hodder & Stoughton Ltd.), p. 252.

> I will turn the darkness before them
>   into light,
>   the rough places into level ground.
>   These are the things I will do,
>   and I will not forsake them (Isaiah 42:16).

In the next chapter God repeats the promise: "I will make a way in the wilderness" (Isaiah 43:19).

It is only human and utterly easy for you and me to conclude that if there is any road at all in the wilderness of our existence, we must have about reached the end of it.

Perplexities confront nations. Complex, tough problems confront our nation. Can the international conferences ever produce a satisfactory solution to incredibly costly and undecisive wars? Are we on the road to fair and just resolution of what is our number one moral problem, our relationships with the nonwhite community? Obstructions seem insuperable.

What of the Christian religion? What of the churches — *the church* itself — in our revolutionary age? Good men and women become discouraged. They become weary of hearing of "the generation gap." Many younger persons and older persons have bridged the gap through understanding. It has been done. But as a society, are we ever likely to bridge the generation gap? Think of the vastness of the problem! In the United States there are forty million young adults. The average age of our population will soon be twenty-four to twenty-five years. There are now approximately ten million university students. What of the apathy to what we would call normal standards of morality? Someone says that in many young adults there is a strain of temporariness. This can be seen in the attitude to marriage. Some will not enter it, although they will live together, for they oppose a permanent bond and binding tie. From this group comes harsh criticism of the church and religion. They say that religion is for older people who have given up living.

Here is an insight which helps me regain perspective: "In the perplexities which confront nations and the church, if God were limited to alternatives which men see we might well be hopeless. It is because he leads the blind *by a way that they know not* that we can be confident." [2] Of course we cannot have a clue as to how God will work out his good purpose in the tomorrows. But we have had rich experience of God's love and care. When Martin Luther's friend Melanchthon hesitated to throw himself into the dangerous work of trying to reform and renew the church, Luther wrote him: "Had Moses waited till he understood how Israel could elude Pharaoh's armies, they might have been in Egypt still." It is when the free nations of mankind and the church in daring trust embark on God's enterprises that the darkness becomes light.

We must unite our confidence in God, our trust in Christ, and in one another, with action that is intelligent, planned, and adventurous. Then we shall know that what may have seemed the end of the road is but a bend in the road.

Much of Isaiah's writing is sublime poetry. Who has not known in the more prosaic experiences of everyday living how a blind alley turned out to be a thoroughfare, and how an apparently hopeless barrier proved to have an open way through it? In the dramatic story of the apostle Peter's liberation from prison told in the twelfth chapter of the Acts of the Apostles, there seems to be almost a touch of magic. The narrative tells how an angel of the Lord — and the Lord uses strange messengers for his delivering angels — broke the chains holding Peter's wrists. *The New English Bible* translates the Greek vividly: "He [Peter] followed him out, with no idea that the angel's intervention was real: he thought it was just a vision. But they passed the first guard-post, then the second, and reached the iron gate leading out into the city, which opened for them of its own accord" (Acts 12:9-10). Peter was "around the bend," free, able to move on to the mission assigned to him. Many Christians could say that when they were sure they had reached the road's end, were at the end of their resources, somehow a way opened up. As Martin Luther is reported to have said, "I was led like an old blind horse." Years ago a popular song gave the sound advice, "Keep right on to the end of the road, keep right on

[2] Henry Sloane Coffin in *The Interpreter's Bible* (Nashville: Abingdon Press, 1956), vol. 5, p. 474.

to the end." When we do keep on, trusting in One who declares that he is the way as well as the truth and the life, we discover that the road's end is not the end, but a way, and that God leads us on.

> I will lead the blind
>   in a way that they know not,
> in paths that they have not known
>   I will guide them.
> I will turn the darkness before them
>   into light,
>   the rough places into level ground (Isaiah 42:16).

Let this hope-filled word of God come to someone. That person may be in a hopsital or nursing home. He may have recovered, but not as completely as he wishes. His birthdays may have accumulated to such a number that he feels he is at the road's end. Remember our Lord Jesus. His enemies thought they could end his life. As the New Testament related, they were ready to destroy him but his time had not yet come (see John 7:6); "he walked straight through them all, and went away" (Luke 4:30, NEB). Arthur Guiterman wrote words for us all:

> My way of life is a winding road,
>   A road that wanders, yet turns not back,
> Where one should go with as light a load
>   As well may be in a traveler's pack.
>
> A road that rambles through marsh and wood,
>   Meadow and waste to the cloudy end;
> But smooth or ridged, I find it good,
>   For something's always around the bend.[3]

Of course what may be coming "around the bend" may seem to be disaster. But wise men and women make provision for future emergencies. The Christian man or woman will face the future without fear. God is there and God is here. A New York clergyman had a parishioner who, past middle age, was informed that his illness would eventually rob him of his sight. He began to study Braille. As darkness descended on

[3] Arthur Guiterman, *Death and General Putnam and 101 Other Poems* (New York: E. P. Dutton & Co., Inc., 1935). Used by permission of Vida Lindo Guiterman.

him, he sank into a deep depression. One day to the surprise of his pastor he returned to the church with a firm step and radiant face. He explained that alone in his room and overwhelmed by hopelessness he had contemplated taking his own life. Flinging his arms across the table, he bowed his head in utter dejection. At that moment he felt Braille letters under his fingers and began to read slowly from the Braille Bible that lay open, "The Lord redeemeth the soul of his servants: and none of them that trust in him shall be desolate."

"It was like a great shaft of light flashed into my darkness," he said. "My depression is gone and I can now face life with trust and confidence knowing that I do not face it alone."

You and I can find resources of hope by reading the Bible, through prayer and worship, and by doing the Christian "thing" with and for others. No completely evil fate will overtake the soul who trusts in God and with God's help does the right. Even when death comes, it need not be the end of the road but a bend in the road, leading to life that shall richer, fuller be.

PRAYER: O God who art our Guide as thou art our Companion, give us faith to go out into today and tomorrow with good courage, not knowing whither we go, but only that thy hand is leading us and thy love is supporting us, through Jesus Christ our Lord. Amen.

Capture our attention, O Lord, that we may receive thy Word and translate it into life, through Christ. Amen.

HOW TO KEEP YOUR ENTHUSIASM

He [Elijah] himself went a day's journey into the wilderness, and came and sat down under a broom tree; but he asked that he might die, saying, "It is enough; . . . I am no better than my fathers" (1 Kings, 19:4).

. . . the stimulus of Christ (Philippians 2:1, Moffatt).

"Half the Adults in America Find Life 'Dull' or 'Routine.'" This headline appeared in the daily newspaper. It was followed by a report of George Gallup, Director, American Institute of Public Opinion, which stated: "Half of U.S. adults interviewed in the latest Gallup Poll find their lives 'dull' or 'pretty routine.'" Interviewers had talked to 1,521 adults in a survey conducted in more than three hundred localities across the country. Respondents represented all walks of life. This question was asked: "In general, do you find life exciting, pretty routine, or dull?"

The report continued: "Those who find life 'dull' mention monotonous jobs, inability to break one's pattern of life, lack of money, infirmity, old age. A fifty-one-year-old woman from Tampa, Florida, who works as a typist, was glum: 'I find life monotonous with never any change. I go to work, come home, go to bed, get up and go to work. I'm alone now — I've raised my son — I guess I'm in a rut.' The majority of those who have lost their zest for living are over the age of fifty. However, a thirty-year-old manual laborer from Los Angeles said: 'Life's dull, because all I do is go to work and come home. My salary covers basic needs but does not give me enough for recreation and relaxation.' "[1]

Highlighted here is a common problem of persons under fifty as well as persons over fifty. It is the problem of how to keep or recover enthusiasm. This is a Christian concern. When we feel low and find life dull and boring, it means that our spirits are low. Anything that concerns our spirits concerns our faith in God. The Gallup survey shows that those who find life dull and unexciting are not regular churchgoers. I believe that there is a definite relation between enthusiasm and a vital Christian faith and practice. Of course everyone, including the most mature Christian, experiences what we once called the "blues" and now call the "blahs." In the Bible there is a character named Elijah. If ever there was a great believer in the living God it was this prophet. Yet when his life was in jeopardy from the malicious, powerful Queen Jezebel, he knew panic and then complete loss of nerve and enthusiasm. Jezebel was out to "get" him and she sent him word of her intention. After a long day's journey into the dark night of his soul, Elijah asked that he might die. "It is enough" (he really meant *it is too much*), "take away my life."

Enthusiasm is one of the keys to effective living. No man or woman succeeds in his profession or business who does not have enthusiasm, however restrained and quiet his personality may be. Could the "amazing Mets," the New York baseball team that won the World Series in 1969, have defeated the excellent Baltimore team without enthusiasm? As for the Christian cause, was anyone ever persuaded that Christ is the answer and that the church is the hope of the world if the Christian he knew best was lukewarm, apathetic, and without enthusiasm for his Lord and for his church?

How do you keep your enthusiasm? How do you maintain zest in living? Someone wrote with twinkling eyes:

[1] *Miami Herald* (October 7, 1969), by permission of the American Institute of Public Opinion (The Gallup Poll).

> A cheerful old bear at the zoo
> Could always find something to do.
> When it bored him to go
> On a walk to and fro,
> He reversed it, and
> Walked fro and to.

But this is no laughing matter. An unknown Christian gives a clue in his observation: "When we look within we are depressed, when we look around we are impressed, when we look at Jesus we are blessed." Reflecting on God's prescription for Elijah, a contemporary Christian leader reduced the formula to three directives: Get up; look up; link up.

God told Elijah to get up. Elijah was flat on his back, wallowing in a stagnant pool of self-pity. He had experienced severe emotional and physical distress. His resources were at an irreducible minimum. He had expended extensive nervous energy in the test on Mount Carmel. He had been one man against 450 hostile men. He was tired and hungry. Then came the frightening message that the queen was determined to get rid of him. After a successful achievement more than one person has been vulnerable. But like the good physician that the Spirit of God is, God said to Elijah, "Get up and eat." He found food and drink available, and after taking them, he slept again. Then the Lord awakened him and told him to eat again, then get moving. He needed to get back into circulation.

One of the great truths which scientific medicine and high religion agree about is that every human being is compounded of body, mind, and spirit. We are neither disembodied spirits nor are we only flesh and blood. We are soul and flesh, bound up together. One man said that the parts of our being are so closely related that they "catch each other's diseases." A well-known minister puts it this way: "When your husband mopes around the house, with the corners of his mouth set at twenty minutes after eight and colors the whole atmosphere with indigo, give him a good lunch and send him out for a game of golf. [I would interpolate: or send him bowling, or fishing, or gardening, or sailing.] The food and exercise will work wonders. And then, when you need it yourself, have the good sense to make the same diagnosis and take the same prescription." [2]

Get up. Then *look up.* God asked Elijah to change his outlook. After his spiritual experience at the mouth of the cave Elijah found his outlook and insight radically different. He learned that God usually speaks, not in the loud phenomena — hurricane wind, earthquake, or fire — but in the still, small voice. How often life seems dull because of our distorted vision! Of course, unexamined optimism is unwarranted; so is unrelieved pessimism. Elijah had surrendered to a debilitating habit of always looking on the dark side. He actually felt sorry for God. He saw many powerful forces lined up against the Almighty! God said in effect: "You are wrong. I have you and a significant company of loyal supporters. There are seven thousand left in Israel who are loyal to the highest." The number "seven thousand" was symbolic, as is "seven" in the Bible. Seven consists of the number "four," which means completion, and "three," which was considered a divine number. For the ancients the perfect number was seven. Elijah was given the message that despite adverse factors there were sufficient assets to turn the tide.

Are you and I thinking the wrong things? Are you holding a dime against one eye and shutting the other, thereby shutting out all light? Are you holding the tough breaks so close to you that you cannot see the bright possibilities? One counselor advised: "When you wake up in the morning try to think of ten good things for which to be thankful." "Then," he said, "your facial clock will move from 8:20 to 10:10"!

A farmer became completely discouraged about his farm. He was discouraged about his house, buildings, land, stock, equipment. At his request a real estate broker put it up for sale and read the farmer his advertising description of the property. "Wait a minute," said the farmer. "Read that again and take it slow." The salesman did. "Changed my mind," said the farmer. "I'm not going to sell. All my life I've been looking for a place like that"!

After you *get up* and *look up, link up* with Christ and

[2] John A. Redhead, *Guidance from Men of God* (Nashville: Abingdon Press, 1965), p. 66.

Christian men and women. Then the Lord will say to you what he said to Elijah.

Do something for others. "What are you doing here, Elijah?" This was the trouble; he was doing nothing. God gave him an assignment. Do you know who finds life dull? Those who do nothing but sit on the sidelines. Those who criticize negatively their church, their community, and their families. At age fifty-five a certain man retired. He thought he would live on his pension and investments. Instead he lived on aches, pains, and grouches. His whole mental occupation was to justify his inactivity; was he not ill? How could he work at anything? Now he is working, not at the job from which he retired, but at something useful. Everybody says he is a different man. He is. Responsibility rested him.

Enthusiasm comes from two Greek words meaning "in God." Or "possessed by God." In God's creative, sustaining Spirit we live. An extraordinary fact about the Christian way of living is the sheer joyous vitality that it brings to life. When D. L. Moody was converted in the shoe store amidst the shoes, he went out and said: "I thought the old sun shone a good deal brighter than it ever had before — I thought it was just smiling upon me, and as I walked across Boston Common and heard the birds singing in the trees, I thought they were all singing a song to me." Years later a young medical student named Wilfred Grenfell was converted under the same evangelism of that same D. L. Moody. Dr. Grenfell, who did so much through his Labrador medical missions, said, "He started me working for all I was worth, and made religion real fun — a new field brimming with opportunities." Life became real fun when life became Christian. If you think our world is going to the dogs, get hold of some part of it which God loves, and help to solve some of the problems and meet some of the needs under what Paul called "the stimulus of Christ."

PRAYER: Enable us, O God, to forget ourselves in serving Christ through serving others. May we get up from any self-absorption, look up to thee, link up with Christ's followers everywhere, and lift up those who need help. Amen.

Quietly, receptively, we would listen for thy Word
to us, in Jesus Christ our Lord. Amen.

IF THIS IS SUNDAY, IT MUST BE HEAVEN!

I was in the Spirit on the Lord's day (Revelation 1:10).

A motion picture comedy had an amusing theme and title. The title could be the exclamation of a bewildered tourist on a packaged travel tour which attempted too much. You know the kind: fourteen airports in twelve days! The title is *If This Is Tuesday, It Must Be Belgium!* (The more thoughtful travel agencies do not recommend this kind of tour.)

Today I dare to affirm in all sincerity, "If this is Sunday, it must be heaven!" It *is* Sunday. But who in their right minds will claim that even a tiny segment of this day is heaven! For Christians, at least for the majority of Christians, Sunday is the Lord's day. Sabbath is observed by our Jewish and Seventh Day Adventist brothers on Saturday. As the Lord's day, the anniversary of his glorious resurrection, Sunday should have something of the quality of heaven here and now. On an island prison off the coast of Asia Minor, the prophet John recalled a heavenly Sunday which he experienced. Concerning it, he wrote, "I was in the Spirit of the Lord's day." To be in the Spirit, in the Spirit of the risen Christ, in the Holy Spirit, is to be in a heavenly state of mind.

"If this is Sunday, it must be heaven!" What is heaven? To most people it is a postmortem place or state of mind, real or imaginary. In the New Testament, heaven is described in such fashion that we know it does not depend on a specific location in space. The pictures of heaven in Scripture are word pictures, not photographs. Christ the Lord is pictured as having ascended "far above all heavens." This suggests that he has transcended all space. The Bible also describes Christians as having been made to abide with Christ "in the heavenly places" (Ephesians 2:6). Heaven is where God is. Heaven is where Christ is. And Christ can be within us as well as among us, here and now.

> Does not Heaven begin that day
> When the eager heart can say,
> Surely God is in this place,
> I have seen Him face to face
> In the loveliness of flowers,
> In the service of the showers,
> And His voice has talked to me
> In the sunlit apple tree.
>   (Bliss Carman in "Here and Now").[1]

But on Sunday? Once it was a holy day, now for the majority it is a holiday. To some it is just another working day. In the far-from-completely-good old days a kind of Old Testament legalism proscribed and prevented innocent, healthful enjoyments such as we take for granted now. Sunday was no day of rest, recreation, and gladness! Frequently, it was a day of gloom, prohibitions, and boredom. An elderly Scottish cousin said to me when I was preparing for the ministry, "David, my lad, can you do anything about Sunday? It's a dreadful day!"

But if this is Sunday, it should be heaven for us!

Come now, some solid citizen protests. Heaven? You are "putting us on" because Sunday does not "turn us on." Heaven? Yes. Sunday can be heavenly and not only because of salubrious weather. A somewhat professionally pious but

---

[1] *Masterpieces of Religions Verse,* edited by James D. Morrison (New York: Harper & Row, Publishers, 1948), p. 451, quoted with permission of McClelland and Stewart Limited.

cheerful clergyman met a parishioner and said, "What a heavenly day! But there, I mustn't talk shop so much!" If this is Sunday, it can have some of heaven's qualities.

Like John, you and I can be in the Spirit on Sunday, for an hour, a half-hour, a few minutes.

Look with me at a few of the ways.

We can engage in the tremendous mystery of encounter with the living God. This encounter is called worship. I like Archbishop William Temple's definition of Christian worship: "To worship is to quicken the conscience with the holiness of God, to feed the mind with the truth of God, to open up the heart to the love of God, to devote the will to the purpose of God."

Harry Emerson Fosdick, one of Protestantism's giants, and a highly critical, nonconformist Christian, once spoke of an experience which he had in a little frame church in New York State. In it, he said, during a simple but real service of worship he passed from the church visible into the church invisible. You need not be a mystic nor a particularly "holy" person to know what such a transforming transaction means. Christ, alive, able to save to the uttermost, can become a present reality.

A second reason why worship gives us a taste of heaven is that *we realize the meaning of the old hymn we sing when we welcome new members: "The fellowship of kindred minds is like to that above."* More than one physician, psychiatrist, and pastor would agree that loneliness is one of the most devastating ailments that afflicts human beings. I am not claiming that taking our place in the communion of the Holy Spirit which is the church at worship and play will provide an instant cure for isolation, depression, and all the other ills we group under the term "loneliness." Nor dare I say that all church members are congenial, understanding, and kind. But it is here, in friendly, affectionate goodwill that we realize that we are "members one of another." When a new contemporary form of worship was introduced into a small Episcopal church in northern Florida, the rector moved down the center aisle taking the hand of each person in an aisle seat in his own. Then the handclasp, symbolic of the Christian kiss of peace, was passed along to everyone in the pew. The minister's greeting was the familiar "The Lord be with you." The layman's response was to be "And with your spirit." A small girl observing this ritual of Christian fellowship was delighted to hear an elderly man who forgot the words respond, "Thank you very much!" Why not? To have the personal interest and Christian love of a fellow soul should evoke gratitude.

There is still another deeper benefit conferred upon us. *It is God's own pardon.* No truly Christian service should omit our need of forgiveness. I know; some secular psychologists decry the church's emphasis on guilt. Nevertheless, even when we use a "general confession" of sin, each of us knows that he is a sinner and needs pardon. Each of us can supply "a bill of particulars." We may not have broken all of the Ten Commandments. It may be a long time since we have flagrantly robbed anyone, or murdered anyone, or tried to deprive him or her of a partner. But have we not committed sins of bad temper, malicious gossip, disloyalty, and mental or other cruelty? What about our sins of omission, the good words we might have said, the good deeds we might have done? George Bernard Shaw had a character in a play say, "The worst sin towards our fellow creatures is not to hate them, but to be *indifferent* to them." Indifference may be a great sin.

Of course we need not wait until Sunday to receive God's forgiveness. But in the church gathered to offer adoration and praise to God, to listen to his word, and to confess sins to him, we may experience the divine acceptance. No audible words from the Lord may be heard, but in our souls we may know he is saying, "Your sins are forgiven. Go and sin no more. Go in peace."

Consider this other heavenly activity: *In our Christian worship we may find vision, inspiration and incentive to follow Christ on the weekdays ahead.* We should be a little less self-centered and a little more sensitive to the needs of others which we can meet with God's help. The church is God's own legion of the compassionate, the great active service force of the concerned. Recently religious journals printed an unexpected tribute to the Christian church. A television correspondent named Stanley Burke of the Canadian Broadcasting Corporation returned from Biafra, in Africa. He gave his highest praise to the church "above all others" for keeping a little country alive and saving at least some of its children from starvation. "When war broke out and Biafra was blockaded, foreigners were asked to leave and they left. All except the missionaries," reported Dr. Francis Ibiam, medical doctor and former World Council president. "We feel they have been a tower of strength to us; they want to suffer with us; they are our friends not only in peacetime, but also in difficulties." Where did such concern grow if not in the living church, through the Holy Spirit operating in responsive minds and spirits?

I am weary of unfounded criticism of the local church and its members. God knows we are not what we should be; but we are better than we were. There is no way to estimate what becomes built into the structures of the weekday world through what goes on in church on Sunday. If only a few who are at worship gain new insights, stronger motivations to do better, and determination to throw the stubborn ounces of their weight on the side of goodness and truth and peace, the results for good are incalculable. A magazine once had an article on "Sermons That Started Something." Among things started were many schools, including Northwestern, Princeton, Yale, Harvard, and Oberlin.

Dr. Crawford Long, of Jefferson, Georgia, one of the pioneers in developing anesthetics, said he got his first idea in church — not from watching people put to sleep! — but by hearing a preacher's text: "The Lord God caused a deep sleep to fall on Adam." He began to wonder how patients could be put to sleep during surgery.

Sermons have stopped things, too, like a war between Chile and Argentina, whose truce produced the famous statue, *The Christ of the Andes*. When Aaron Burr shot Alexander Hamilton in a duel, an Albany, New York, preacher set in motion the initial law which stopped dueling in the United States. Harriet Beecher Stowe got the idea for *Uncle Tom's Cabin* during a communion service. She walked home holding back her tears and then began to write her famous book.

Yes, if this is Sunday, it could be heaven in our life-changing experience of God, in our communion with Christ, in renewal through companionship with our fellow-seekers and fellow-finders, in God's assurance that we are forgiven, accepted, and loved, in the Word — the orders — received whereby we move out into the world of weekday needs and agonies to give Christian service to help make possible needed changes in society. Let me paraphrase Isaiah: "In the year 1971 when much seemed to have perished that we counted precious, I saw the Lord, high and lifted up, tenderly near; and his glory filled the temple; and I confessed my sin, for I am a man of unclean thoughts and unclean words and deeds, living among people also stained and sinful. God himself cleansed me of all my guilt and stain. Then I heard a voice saying through the Scripture, the prayers, the sermon, and the music, 'Whom shall I send and who will go for me?' And I said, 'Lord, here am I. I'm not much but I'm all I've got. Send me. Use me!' "

PRAYER: Lord, we are in the Spirit on the Lord's day. We marvel how God gives us heaven here and now. Send us out to make earth a little more like the kingdom of heaven, through Christ Jesus our Lord. Amen.

> O Holy Spirit, re-collect our thoughts. Face us
> toward Christ. Come to us as truth, as power, as
> love, for thy love's sake. Amen.

YOU DO NOT WALK ALONE

Jesus himself drew near and went with them (Luke 24:15).

You are no longer strangers and sojourners [outsiders, exiles, migrants and aliens, excluded from the rights of citizens], but you are fellow citizens with the saints and members of the household of God (Ephesians 2:19).

You do not walk alone.

Make that statement to many persons today and they would strongly disagree. If you had their confidence and they were completely candid, the answer might be: "But I do walk alone, as you put it. I live alone, ever since my parents (or my husband, or my wife, or my closest friend) died. I live alone, even though I live with others. Since I retired from business, or from my profession, I have been increasingly alone." You listen to older persons and you may hear them say, "Perhaps it is the busyness of modern life for young people, perhaps it is the speed of change that divides the generations, but although we have children and grandchildren, we are more and more alone." You listen to a young person, perhaps a young wife and mother: "I do have my husband and children, but I am alone much of the time. Perhaps I'm not exactly a trapped suburban housewife, but my husband has to be away much of the time. Yes, of course we have good neighbors, and the PTA, and clubs, but the rat race leaves little time to cultivate really deep friendships. Then, we move quite often." Other younger citizens have come to the city from smaller communities for opportunity, education, entertainment, and independence, and they find no substitute for the sense of community they had back home. Sometimes loneliness stems from desertion, rejection, or rebellion. It is curious that in our age with improved communications, travel, socializing, and community centers, so many feel that they walk and live alone. T. S. Eliot, in one of his "Choruses from 'The Rock'" points to the core of our condition:

> And now you live dispersed on ribbon roads,
> And no man knows or cares who is his neighbour
> Unless his neighbour makes too much disturbance,
> But all dash to and fro in motor cars,
> Familiar with the roads and settled nowhere.[1]

There is a kind of loneliness, of course, which is the price of a sensitive, enlightened conscience; a loneliness which is the price of leadership, consecration, and sacrifice. Our Scriptures show that God needed to get men alone to deal with them. For example, there were Abraham, Jacob, and Moses in the wilderness and on the mount, John in the desert, Paul's virtually unshared spiritual experience on the Damascus road, and the prophet John on Patmos. We would agree that man's loneliness is often God's opportunity.

Nevertheless, this kind of loneliness is more like solitude, marked by an uncrowded life. At its most creative depths, this solitariness shines with awareness of God's companionship. Said Jesus in such aloneness, "The Father is with me. . . . He who sent me is with me; he has not left me alone" (John 16:32; 8:29).

What does the gospel say to those who feel the burden and heartache of being alone? This is the good news: *You do not walk alone. You need not walk alone.*

[1] T. S. Eliot, "Choruses from 'The Rock'" in *The Complete Poems and Plays of T. S. Eliot* (Harcourt, Brace, Jovanovich, Inc., 1952), p. 102.

First, *you do not walk alone as you realize your oneness with other members of the human race.* In 1 Samuel 25:29, Abigail uses a memorable phrase for a fact of human existence. She is reassuring the king that all will be well with him even if his enemies are chasing him to destroy him. She says, "If men rise up to pursue you and to seek your life, the life of my lord shall be bound in the bundle of the living in the care of the Lord your God."

This sublime truth is for each one of us: we are bound together in the bundle of the living, in the care of the Lord our God. But we commonly act as if we were isolated, fragmented, unrelated atoms. We have a phrase for it: we are loners. Then we isolate ourselves from others, drawing back because of superficial differences. Loneliness becomes a vicious circle. We become resentful, and our friendlessness becomes unfriendliness. A few years ago in the heart of the city of London, Dr. Leslie Weatherhead, then minister of the City Temple, was asked to speak on the subject of friendship. In the new postwar building of the City Temple, the chapel is named The Chapel of the Divine Friendship. He treated loneliness as an evil thing, agreeing with a psychiatrist that it is "one of the major social evils of our day." Dr. Weatherhead suggested practical things that a man or woman, a boy or girl, can do to cure the disease of loneliness. One suggestion was that the lonely person face the question: "Is my loneliness my own fault?" A novelist described a woman called Edith in what may have been cruel terms: "Edith is a very small island, bounded on the north, on the south, on the east, and on the west, by Edith." There some persons who have made the wonderful discovery that the way to be loved is to love. The way to be visited is to visit, or to invite people who may not be able to invite you back. The way to experience companionship is to join a company of good companions, as a volunteer in a good cause. The way to lose loneliness is to engage in some service for others. If a person is left alone, he must make a positive and continuous effort to make new friends, not simply wait to be visited or called upon.

Is this all we can say in support of the claim, "You do not need to walk alone"? Far from it. Obviously, *we need never be alone because we have God for our Friend.* But this is an abstract idea for most people until somehow it is warmed up by human love that makes us sure that love is divine. The great philosopher and mathematician, Dr. Alfred North Whitehead, said that "religion is what you do with your solitariness." A thoughtful reader of Whitehead's aphorism suggests that it sounds even better the other way round: "What one does with solitariness is — religion."

The awareness of divine love even in solitariness is certainly the religion of Jesus Christ. Jesus came to call men into community, into deep, dynamic, intimate fellowship, the fellowship of God's love. "He sought out the lonely: the woman coming alone to draw water, the blind man avoiding crowds in the city, Zaccheus the ostracized, the leper debarred from all society, the one man left at the Pool of Siloam, the grieving Peter; and the promise, 'I will not leave you desolate' is for all whose lives have fallen in solitary places. The more that He Himself was rejected and thrust out and forced to stand and suffer alone, the more He strove to bind His men in loyalty and fellowship, in service and a remembering Communion that should make the Church one through all generations. And His final, unforgettable words were on this theme: 'Lo, I am with you — always.' "[2]

In the last chapter of Luke's Gospel there is a report which has far wider and timeless application than the original intention of the author: "While they were talking and discussing together, Jesus himself drew near and went with them." How often the living Christ goes unrecognized! But he is as near as our need. Recall what the mechanic said to the explorer Shackleton when they finished their terrible journey, "Boss, I had a feeling we were not three but four." Eight centuries ago Bernard of Clairvaux wrote that while Christ visited him he never knew when he came. How did he know he was present? "In the renovation and reformation of my mind and spirit . . . I have seen the fashion of His beauty." You may not be a mystic, and you may distrust mysticism. But have you not sensed now and then a Presence beside you — not a

[2] Reginald E. O. White, *A Relevant Salvation* (Grand Rapids, Mich.: Wm. B. Eerdmans Publishing Co., 1963), pp. 32-33.

"spook" but a Savior, Lord, and Friend? Christianity began in friendship. Like any true friend, Christ stabs our conscience broad awake. He accompanies us when we enter a voting booth. He compels us to choose as wisely as we know how. Edwin Booth, famed actor, was once asked by a timid clergyman if there was a side door through which he could slip in to see a performance, unseen by any narrow parishioners. Said Booth, "There is no door into my theater through which God cannot see."

You *need never walk alone if you belong to the true community around Jesus Christ.* To many persons Booth's assertion may sound lovely but unreal, religious but remote. They might agree that Christianity could be defined (as indeed it has been by Leslie Weatherhead) as "the acceptance of Christ's friendship." But how can anyone experience friendship with One, however great, however loving and lovable, who lived more than nineteen centuries ago? Granted, if Christ was raised from the dead, if the Resurrection story is true, then somehow Christ must be alive now. It is here that the necessity of the church comes in. We believe, says the Apostles' Creed, in the holy, catholic [or universal] Church. We believe in the communion of saints. Christ gives us this community, a community of faith in which men and women and children realize that they belong to God and to one another; a community in which they are accepted regardless of their racial origin, past history, or failures and sins. This is a community of fellowship where we bear each other's burdens, rejoice with those who do rejoice, and weep with those who weep. This is the community where we find release from the prison of the moment into the unbroken communion of saints.

Now the declaration of the apostle in the second chapter of his letter to the Ephesian Christians comes alive: "You are no longer strangers and sojourners, but you are fellow citizens with the saints and members of the household of God." Paul is saying to the Gentiles, "You are no longer in the church and among God's people on a kind of alien resident's visa. You are real citizens of God's kingdom. You are full members of the family of God." This is why no congregation of the great church can be more exclusive than God. There is no community to compare with the deeply-rooted, world-encircling fellowship of hearts made one in the love of Christ. But membership of the saints is more than just a worldwide association. It spans the centuries as well.

Look at that word "saint." The connotation of the word is not always appealing. A high-school boy said, "I don't want to be a saint; I want to be a real guy." When you hear the word "saint," what comes into your mind? A pious soul, an uncongenial "do-gooder," or as they once said irreverently in college circles, a "Christer"? But the New Testament concept of a saint is not of one officially canonized, or personally over-pious, or overbearingly virtuous. The root meaning of the word translated "saint" is "holy," complete, as we would describe one on the way to wholeness, to completion of personality. But in the New Testament church a saint was not just a holy person; he was one who had committed himself to Jesus Christ as Lord and Savior and had become part of the community whose members shared in new spiritual power and grace. Interestingly enough, out of sixty-two references to the saints in the New Testament, the singular word "saint" occurs only once. There could not be any individual saints in the early church. Someone has said, truly, "As there can be no human being who does not share in the breathing of air, so there can be no saint who does not share in the fellowship of those whose lives are filled with the love of Christ." A saint is a Christian on the way to Christlikeness. To Paul, becoming a Christian meant not only believing in and trusting Jesus Christ but, above all, becoming a member of the community whose chief aim was to follow Christ in all of life. We are all sinners, but because we are dedicated to follow Christ we belong to the fellowship, the communion of saints.

We have communion, meeting, sharing, and participation with saints. Haven't we all had the experience of meeting someone and suddenly "clicking"? We say we are on the same wave-length. We communicate with each other. You and I need never be alone because we participate in the communion of saints. We belong to a great unseen society of those in the past, the present, and the future who are joined together through the sharing of the love, grace, and Spirit of Jesus Christ. We talk about ecumenical councils. The communion of saints is the most ecumenical society in the world. In it are the Abrahams and Joshuas, the Isaiahs and Jeremiahs and Amoses, the Pauls and Peters, the Francises and Martin Luthers, the John Wesleys and John Calvins, the Albert Schweitzers and Tom Dooleys, the David Livingstones and dear men and women of every day who are cheering for us and (who knows?) helping us on.

You and I do not walk alone. We are bound together in the bundle of the living in the care of the Lord our God. As we walk, Jesus himself draws near and goes with us. We are, through Christ, "fellow citizens with the saints and members of the household of God."

PRAYER: O thou who art the Father of our spirits and the lover of all souls, we join in thy church's thanksgiving for all the shining company of thy saints. Especially would we thankfully remember those whom our own eyes have seen in the beauty of goodness. We thank thee that in them thou hast permitted us to see something of what thou canst do for those who commit themselves to thee and to thy Son our Lord, Jesus Christ. Keep us in loving fellowship with them, that being close to them we may be not far from thee. In Jesus Christ our Lord. Amen.

Let new light break forth from thy Word, O God,
that we may be thankful. In Christ. Amen.

WHAT DO YOU TAKE LIFE FOR?

Jesus remarked, "Weren't there ten men healed? Where are the other nine? Is nobody going to turn and praise God for what has been done, except this stranger?" (Luke 17:17-18, Phillips).

A witty commentator on the human scene made an interesting observation. He said that there are two kinds of people in the world: those who divide the world into two kinds of people, and those who do not. Preachers commonly like to divide a subject or text into three parts. One of my friends is a most effective preacher and a sermon-builder. From him I borrow three categories or kinds of response to life made by men and women such as ourselves. My friend must not be blamed for the use I made of these categories! They describe the main responses human beings make to the question: What do you take life for?

There are those who take life for granted. The large majority of the lepers healed by Jesus did this. In the days when this dreaded disease received no effective treatment, no alleviation or cure, ten victims came to the great Physician. Jesus was always fighting disease and sickness since he was sure it originated in the mysterious evil forces he branded as Satan.

Nine of the men who were healed took their renewed life and their restored health for granted. They never returned to say as much as "Thank you." Then, says Dr. Luke, who would have professional interest in this marvelous cure and sequel, "Jesus remarked (after only one of the ten cured patients returned to give thanks, and this one a despised, ostracized Samaritan): 'Weren't there ten men healed? Where are the other nine? Is nobody going to turn and praise God for what has been done, except this stranger?'" (Luke 17:17-18, Phillips). Jesus was astonished that only one of the group thanked God.

Why are we ungrateful? Because we have so much and consider that life owes us the good gifts? Probably. The Bible suggests in one of its psalms that we are frequently ungrateful because we are forgetful. "Forget not all his benefits," the Scripture reminds us (Psalm 103:2). It is an appropriate season to retell the story of the young man on a crowded bus who decided to give up his seat to a young lady. When the lady realized what was happening, she was so surprised that she fainted! As soon as she came to, looking up at the young man who had given her his seat, she said, "Thank you!" Then he was so surprised that he fainted! Yes, one of life's mysteries is why so many otherwise nice people are ungrateful.

All of us live in a world that does not belong to us, that has been bought with a price that we did not and cannot pay. No member of a local church pays for all that he receives from it. Who can pay for Christ on the cross? Who can pay for the presence of the loving Spirit, the unfailing Order, the supporting Power we call God? Who can buy the prayer of a St. Francis such as the one which begins: "Lord, make me an instrument of thy peace"? For Martin Luther's witness to essential New Testament Christianity? John Calvin's emphasis on the sovereign grace of God? John Wesley's evangelistic endeavors which brought two continents nearer to the feet of Christ? Charles Wesley's and Isaac Watts' hymns? The music of Johann Sebastian Bach, Handel, and all the other master musicians, ancient and modern? For Pilgrims kneeling at Plymouth Rock? For the missionaries who brought Christianity to our ancestors?

What student pays for all the worth he receives at college or university? As for our country, and our heritage, who can pay for frozen troops at Valley Forge? The wounds and deaths at Ypres, the Somme, the Marne? Bataan, Salerno, Normandy? Heartbreak Hill in Korea? The thousands of wounded and killed boys in Vietnam? The Industrial Revolution? For the Constitution, born out of storm and stress? Who can pay for things that are to be seen daily wherever one lives, such as the rhythm of ocean waves, the sunrise and sunset, the mountainlike clouds with trees silhouetted against crimson skies? Yes, Shakespeare spoke truly when he had King Lear say in the time of his own tragedy:

> How sharper than a serpent's tooth it is
> To have a thankless child!

Everyday we live finds us wearing clothes we did not make, eating food we did not produce, using gadgets we did not invent, profiting by laws we did not pass, reaching toward ideals we did not originate.

What do we take life for? *Some take life for griping.* But are there not such things as bad luck, unlucky breaks, undeserved tragedy, and blasted hopes in human experience? Of course there are. Why jump up and down for joy when you face the grim realities? No one, least of all a Christian, is supposed to wax ecstatic over that which is tragic. But why magnify the sombre aspects out of all proportion? Did you ever have someone show you a large sheet of white paper or cardboard on one side of which a tiny black dot was made? "What do you see?" asks the holder of the paper. Invariably the answer comes, "I see a black dot!" Never, "I see a large expanse of white paper." The black dot is not all there is. Without expanses of white we would never see the black dot! Dr. Ralph W. Sockman is well known as a Sunday afternoon radio preacher with a continental congregation. In mid-career of his great ministry in New York City, Mrs. Sockman and he suffered the tragic death of their only son. Soon after, Dr. Sockman wrote: "Speaking personally, may I say that during the last decade of my life things have happened to me that I cannot explain, nor can I say they were all sent of God.

When I read, 'All things work together for good for them that love God,' the only way I can understand this in my own case is after the analogy of a ship. There are parts of a ship which taken by themselves would sink. The engine would sink. The propeller would sink. But when the parts of a ship are built together, they float. So with the events of my life. Some have been tragic. Some have been happy. But when they are built together, they form a craft that floats. Aye, more, one that I believe is going somewhere. And I am comforted." I have also been helped by this sentence by an unknown Christian philosopher: "Some persons grumble because God placed thorns among roses. Why not thank God he placed roses among thorns?"

Some of God's children take life for granted. Others take life for griping, and if you have to work with them in a home, in an office, or in a church you sometimes wish that they would take a one-way trip to the moon! Thank God, *there are those who take life for gratitude!*

A church member told me of something his church in Illinois did around Thanksgiving Day. The pastor asked every member to write a note saying "thank you" to at least one person for something precious, seal the letter, stamp it, and then on the Sunday before Thanksgiving Day bring it to church. All letters were collected by the ushers, blessed at the communion table, and mailed. It is a good idea.

What am I thankful for? So much, that it is accurate to say that it is more than tongue can tell. For life, and the opportunities for spiritual growth and adventures in service; for the love and loyalty of my wife with whom it is as easy to stay in love as it was to fall in love; for children and grandchildren whose affection enhances the joy of living; for health and for friends; for the holy catholic or universal church, and for the church that I serve; for the men and women who called me to its ministry, and for the support of ninety-nine and forty-four hundredths percent of the members! For the men and women who helped found the congregation and for those pioneers who are still among us; for the new members who have strengthened our witness and worship; for our country; for responsible freedom within the context of just laws; for

the freedom to dissent peaceably from what we consider to
be unfair or untrue to the will of God; above all, for our
great salvation bought with so great a price by the God of
holy love in Jesus Christ; for Christ's spiritual companionship
— for all these I give thanks.

Today many sing a great hymn of thanksgiving. It was
written by Pastor Martin Rinkart and published in the year
1647. His village of Eilenberg, Saxony, had been devastated
by a plague followed by famine in the year 1637. In one year
eight thousand persons perished. In one year Pastor Rinkart
conducted four thousand burial services. When the sickness
abated, Martin Rinkart wrote the great hymn:

> Now thank we all our God
>   With heart and hands and voices,
> Who wondrous things hath done,
>   In whom His world rejoices;
> Who, from our mothers' arms,
>   Hath blessed us on our way
> With countless gifts of love,
>   And still is ours today.

PRAYER: Glad are we that we live in thy world and in thy
grace, O God. May we show forth our thanks "not only with
our lips but in our lives, by giving up ourselves to thy service
and by walking before thee in holiness and righteousness all
our days," through Jesus Christ our Lord.

Unto God's gracious mercy and protection we commit ourselves and all whom we love and all the children of God. The
grace of the Lord Jesus Christ, and the love of God, and the
communion of the Holy Spirit be with us all. Amen.